Heritage Holidays

Recall your own family heritage with authentic antique postcard designs and antique style papers used for the page background and photo frames. Black and white photos spin nostalgic tales of yesteryear.

See How to Make a Spinner Page on page 6

Turn the Spinner to see the page title in the camera.

Turn the Spinner to see photo 1.

Turn the Spinner again to see photo 2.

Turn the Spinner again to see photo 3.

MATERIALS: Design Originals 12" papers (*#0415 Wallpaper on Sepia, #0416 Diamonds on Ivory, #0417 Floral on Green, #0410 Seasonal Postcards, #0411 Letter Postcards*) • Cardstock (Ivory) • Camera cut-out • Paper brad • Deckle scissors for photos

INSTRUCTIONS:

Page. Use a full sheet of *Floral on Green* paper.

Spinner. Trim *Diamonds on Ivory* paper to 11" square. Cut a camera from *Wallpaper on Sepia*. Glue camera on *Diamonds on Ivory* paper. Cut a 2½" opening in the center of the camera.

Spinner Wheel - Cut an 8½" circle of Ivory cardstock with wavy-edge scissors. Punch a hole in the center of Spinner. Place Spinner behind the camera and punch a small hole through *Diamonds on Ivory*. Insert brad and flatten to secure. Trim photos into circles, position under the camera hole, remove wheel and glue photos on Ivory wheel. Glue *Diamonds on Ivory* on top of the *Floral on Green,* leaving the edge of Spinner wheel free.

Photos. Cut *Wallpaper on Sepia* into a 5" square and a 3¼" x 4¼" rectangle. Trim photos with deckle scissors.

Scallop Frame. Cut 2 scallop shapes following the design in *Wallpaper on Sepia*. Glue on each side of 5" square.

Finish. Cut postcards from decorative paper. Mount scallop shapes, mats, photos and postcards on page as shown.

Spinner Photo Wheel

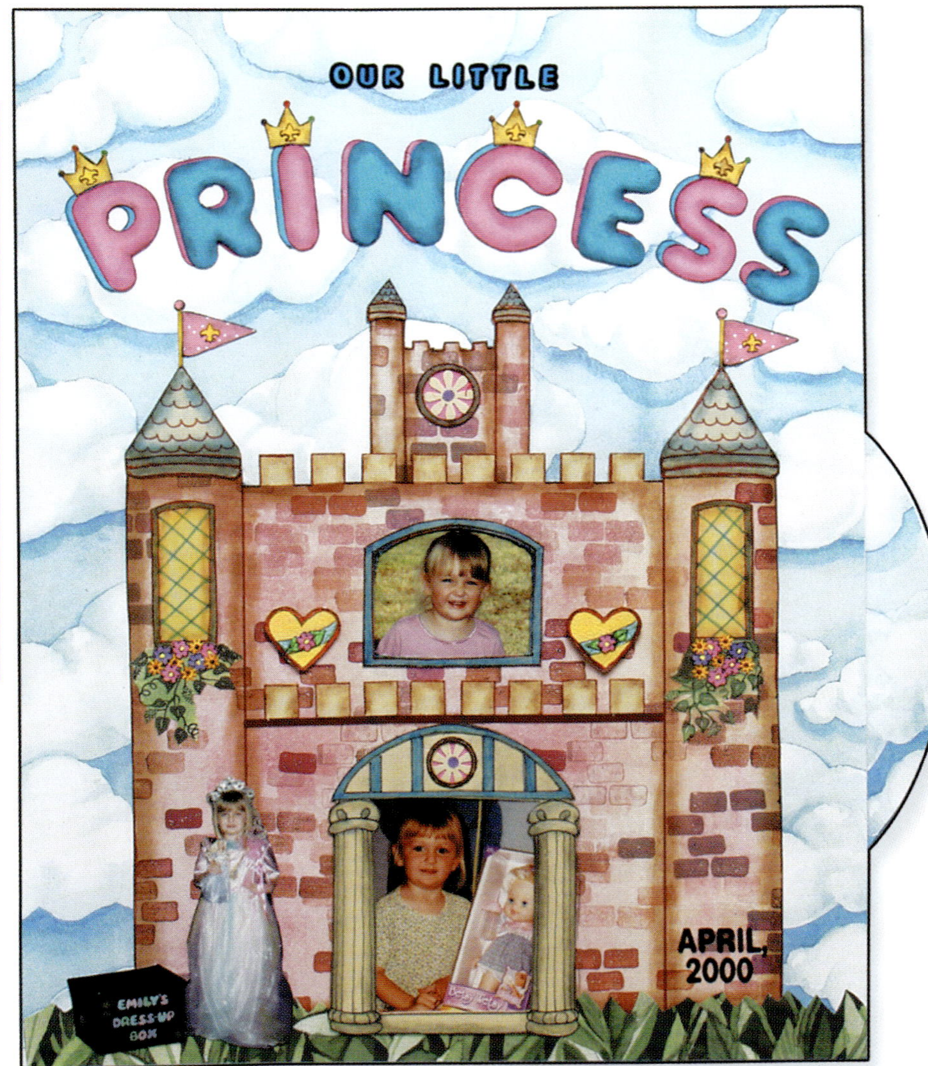

Every princess deserves her own castle. Add photos to a spinner and she will think she is 'The Queen'.

Our Little Princess

MATERIALS: Design Originals 12" papers (2 *#0397 Sky & Clouds, #0424 Home Style Bricks, #0399 Garden Leaves*) • 12" Cardstock (White, Tan, Yellow, Pink, Turquoise, Purple, Burgundy) • Punches (1⁄8", 1⁄2", 5⁄8", 3⁄4" and 1 1⁄4" Circle; 3⁄4" Heart; 3⁄8" Square; 5⁄8" Flower; 1⁄2" Primitive Heart; 1⁄2" Crown; Fleur de Lis Border; Flower Border; Celebration Border) • 1 1⁄4" letters template • Letter stickers (1⁄4" Turquoise, 3⁄8" Black) • Gel pens (Brown, Blue, Gray, Green, Black, Red, Burgundy) • Chalk (Gray, Brown) • Jumbo deckle scissors • Pop dots • Paper brad

INSTRUCTIONS:

Page. Trim *Sky & Cloud* paper to fit page.

Castle. Cut castle from *Brick*. Glue castle on trimmed *Sky* paper. Punch 16 Tan cardstock squares. Outline with Brown pen and shade with Brown chalk. Glue across top and center of castle as shown. Cut a 1⁄8" x 4 3⁄4" Burgundy cardstock strip. Glue below squares on center of castle. Cut a 1" strip of *Leaves*, trim with deckle scissors and glue on bottom.

Cut center window from Turquoise cardstock. Cut opening in window with a craft knife. Place center window on castle, trace opening on page and cut out.

Wheel. Glue *Sky* paper on White cardstock. Cut a 7 1⁄2" circle. Cut 5 photos larger than the center window, glue on wheel. Make a hole in the center of window and page. Attach wheel to page with a brad. Crop 4 round photos and glue on wheel.

Windows & Doors. Glue center window frame over opening. Cut doorway and side windows from Tan. Cut opening in doorway. Crop photo to fit doorway, glue together and on castle. Silhouette photo and glue on side of castle. Glue side windows in place.

Punch 1⁄2" and 5⁄8" circles from Pink and Gray cardstock. Repunch Gray circles with 5⁄8" and 3⁄4" circles. Punch 2 Tan flowers. Layer and glue together. Trim edges. Punch 1⁄8" Lavender circles for flower centers. Glue on castle.

Castle Trim. Cut ivy from *Brick* and glue under side windows. Punch 2 Yellow hearts. Detail with pens and chalk. Punch assorted colors of flowers and cut 4 leaves from ivy. Glue flowers and leaves on hearts. Glue flowers on ivy. Draw flower centers with pens. Glue one heart to top of brad and attach other heart to page with a pop dot.

Cut roofs from Tan cardstock. Detail with pen and chalk then glue in place. Punch 2 Pink primitive hearts for flags, cut off rounded ends. Cut 1⁄8" Yellow cardstock strips for poles. Glue poles and flags on page. Punch 1⁄8" Pink circles, glue on top of poles. Punch 2 Yellow fleur de lis, glue on flags.

Title. Punch 1 1⁄4" Pink and Turquoise circles. Using a template, cut puffy letters from circles. Assemble letters and shade with Gray chalk. Glue on page. Punch 4 crowns and 4 fleur de lis from Yellow cardstock. Glue together and above letters. Outline with a Black pen and shade with chalk. Draw jewels with pens. Apply Turquoise letter stickers and date with Black stickers.

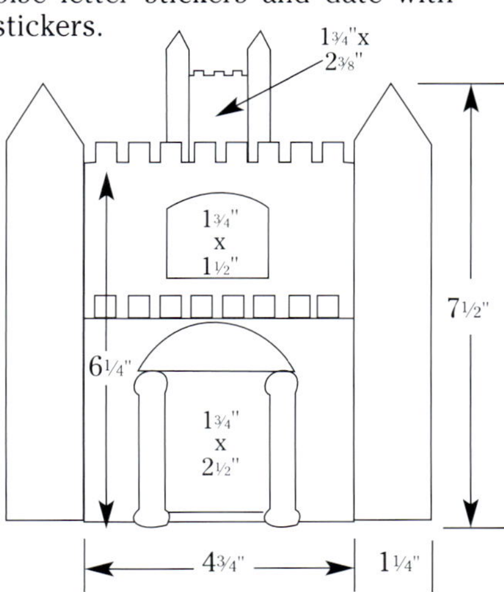

Turn the wheel to see additional photos!

Turn the Spinner Wheel to see more photos!

Bubbling with fun, this page lets you spin through photos of water babies at play.

Water Fun

MATERIALS: Design Originals 12" papers (*#0401 Deep Blue Sea, #0398 Water & Swirls, #0422 Beach & Sunny Sky*) • Clear Vellum • 12" Cardstock (White, Black, Yellow, Red, Orange, Green, Lime Green, Tan, Brown, Flesh) • Punches (3/16", 5/16", 1/2", 5/8", 3/4", 1", 1 1/4", 1 1/2", 2" and 2 7/8" Circle; 1/2" Shell; 1/2" Oval; 1/4" and 5/8" Fish; 1 1/8" Smiley; 1/2" Tropical Fish; 5/8" Seahorse; 1 5/8" Grass; Swirl Border #1; Swirl Border #2) • 1 1/4" letter template • Letter stickers (5/16" Red, Black) • Gel pens (Black, Yellow, White, Blue) • Chalk (Blue, Pink) • Paper brad

INSTRUCTIONS:

Page. Cut 2 Yellow 1 1/4" wide cardstock strips and glue on *Sea* paper as borders.

Swimmer. Cut a wave from *Water & Swirls* paper, goggles from Red cardstock and Vellum, 2 hands from Flesh, snorkel from Lime Green and Yellow cardstock. Cut a Flesh 3" circle head. Punch 2 Black 3/16" circles for eyes and a Smiley for the mouth. Punch hair from Brown and Light Brown cardstock using swirl border punches. Punch White 5/16", 1/2", 3/4", 1" and 1 1/4" circles for bubbles. Outline shapes with Black pen, color details with pens and shade with chalk. Assemble swimmer and glue bubbles on wave. Reserve one small bubble. Glue swimmer on *Deep Blue Sea*.

Spinner. Punch 3 White 1 1/2" cardstock circles. Repunch with 2" circles to make frames. Place middle frame on page, trace and cut an opening in page. Glue *Water & Swirls* on White cardstock, cut a 7 1/2" circle. Make holes in wheel and page. Crop 5 photos into 2" circles and glue on wheel. Attach wheel with a brad. Glue reserved bubble on brad. Crop additional photos into 2" circles, glue behind frames and glue frames on page. Glue *Deep Blue Sea* page on album page, leaving Spinner wheel free.

Title. Cut 2 1/2" x 9 1/2" Red and 2 1/4" x 9 1/2" Light Blue cardstock strips. Glue on top of page. Cut letters from *Water Swirls* paper and White cardstock. Outline with Black pen. Glue letters together. Using border punches, punch swirls and punch shells from *Beach & Sunny Sky* paper. Punch fish and seahorses from cardstock referring to photo for colors. Outline shapes and details with pens. Glue title as shown.

Journaling. Punch a 2" White cardstock circle, outline with Black pen and shade with Blue chalk. Apply stickers and write 'at the' with Black pen. Glue on page.

How to Make a Spinner Page

Page Preparation. Glue cardstock or background paper on album page. Plan shape and position of decorative page element. Use a circle template to trace shape on cardstock. Cut out. Place element on page and trace opening. Cut an opening in the page. Glue element on page.

Wheel. Use a ruler to measure size of circle needed. Cut circle from cardstock. (Or glue background paper on cardstock and cut out.) Use a pointed instrument to punch a small hole at the exact center of wheel. Place wheel behind opening in album page. Turn page over. Make a hole through wheel hole into page. Thread paper brad through holes in page and wheel. Spread brad ends to secure.

Photos. Crop photos slightly larger than the shape of page opening. Determine placement by turning wheel and lightly tracing around opening with a pencil Remove wheel. Glue photos in place. Glue stickers or punched shapes between photos if desired. Refasten wheel. Turn wheel to check placement of photos.

Finish. Place a second album page behind the first page, sandwiching the wheel. Glue edges of pages together leaving the wheel free to turn. Punch a 1/4" circle from matching paper and glue on brad. Glue remaining elements on page. Add title and journaling.

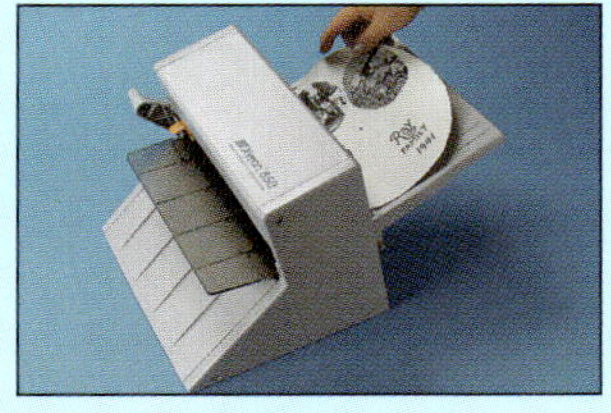

Page Protectors. Protect pages from sticky fingers. Laminate the wheel (with photos attached) on a Xyron. Place the wheel behind the page, then secure with the brad. Place page on top of a page protector. Use scissors to make a slit in the side of the page protector where the wheel is positioned. Slip the page inside the page protector. Position wheel thru slit.

Punch cardstock as follows:

Sandcastle.
9 Tan - 3/8" Squares
3 Brown - 1" Ovals
Pink - 1/2" Primitive Heart
Yellow - Fleur de Lis Border

Boy in Tube.
Tan - 1 3/4" Doll
Purple - 1" Romper
8 Brown - 1/4" Suns
2 Turquoise - 1/4" Ovals
Yellow Vellum - 1" Oval

Girl in Bikini.
Peach - 1 3/4" Doll
Orange - 5/8" Circle
2 Orange - 3/8" Birch Leaves
2 Yellow Vellum - 5/16" Ovals
2 Black 1/8", 2 Pink 1/4" Hearts
Turquoise - 5/8" Heart

Girl in Sundress.
Peach - 1 3/4" Doll
Pink Print - 1" Dress
Brown - 5/8" Circle
2 Brown - 3/8" Birch Leaves
2 White - 1/4" Bows
Yellow - 1/4" Duck

Girl in Sunsuit.
Peach - 1 3/4" Doll
Pink Print - 1" Overalls
Yellow - 5/8" Circle
Yellow - 7/8" Bell
Pink - 1/8" Heart
2 Black - 1/8" Heart
Blue and 2 White 1/4" Heart

Girl in Grass Skirt.
Tan - 1 3/4" Doll
Black - 5/8" Cloud
2 Black - 3/4" Black Oak Leaf
3 Pink - 1/4" Flowers
Brown - 1/2" Rectangle
Green - 1 1/4" Sun
Turquoise - 1/2" Circle
Yellow - 5/8" Circle
Pink - Flower Corner

Boy with Lei.
Tan - 1 3/4" Doll
Turquoise Print - 1" Romper
Brown - 1/2" Rectangle
Black - 1/4" Sun
Green - 1" Sun
Black - 5/8" Circle
Pink - Flower Corner
2 Purple - Flower Corners
2 Yellow - Flower Corners

Boy in Overalls.
Peach - 1 3/4" Doll
Purple Print - 1" Overalls
12 Brown - 1/4" Suns
2 Green - 3/16" Stars
2 Black - 3/16" Stars
Pink - City Lights Corner

PLACE ON FOLD

SANDCASTLE PATTERN

Bring back the smell of fresh breezes, the warmth of the sand and the sound of the waves on a beach with a sandcastle page spinning with photos.

At the Beach

MATERIALS: Design Originals 12" papers (2 *#0422 Beach & Sunny Sky, Pink Print, Turquoise Print, Purple Print*) • Yellow Vellum • 12" Cardstock (White, Black, Brown, Orange, Yellow, Tan, Peach, Pink, Green, Turquoise, Purple, Pale Gold) • Punches (1¾" Doll; 1" Overalls; 1" Romper; 1" Dress; ½" and ⅝" Circle; ⅛", ¼" and ⅝" Heart; ¼", 5⁄16" and 1" Oval; ½" Primitive Heart; ¼", 1" and 1¼" Sun; ⅜" Birch Leaf; ⅜" Square; ¾" White Oak Leaf; ⅝" Cloud; ¼" Bow; 5⁄16" Duck; 3⁄16" Star; ¼" Flower; ⅞" Bell; ¼" Rectangle; Fleur de Lis Border; City Lights Corner; Flower Corner) • Oval template • Letter stickers (5⁄16" Black) • Die-cut letters (White, Turquoise) • 3" die-cut frames (Turquoise, Yellow) • Gel pens (Brown, Gold, Black) • Chalk (Gray, Brown, Pink) • Colored pencils • Pop dots • Paper brad

INSTRUCTIONS:

Page. Trim one sheet of *Beach* paper to fit and glue on album page. Cut one starfish from *Beach* paper, glue on sand.

Sandcastle. Cut a 6½" slit along edge of sand on bottom of *Beach* paper starting ⅝" from right side to hold sandcastle and doll feet. Cut sandcastle from Pale Gold cardstock using pattern. Insert castle in slit and glue in place leaving top free. Punch 9 Pale Gold ⅜" squares, glue as shown. Cut 2⅝" oval through sandcastle and page.

Wheel. Glue *Beach* paper on White cardstock and cut an 8¾" circle. Make a hole through center of wheel and left side of sandcastle. Crop 4 oval photos and glue on wheel. Attach wheel to page with a brad. Glue second page behind first, leaving the wheel free.

Sandcastle Trim. Punch 3 Brown 1" ovals, trim. Outline with Brown pen and shade with Brown chalk. Glue 2 on sandcastle and one on brad. Secure with pop dots to make windows. Outline sandcastle with Gold pen and shade with Brown chalk. For flag, cut a 1⁄16" Brown strip, Punch a Pink primitive heart and Yellow fleur de lis. Outline with Black pen and shade Gray. Glue as shown for flag.

Dolls. Punch dolls and clothing referring to photo for colors and placement. Embellish with gel pens and chalk. Glue 3 dolls on bottom of page, sliding the feet of 2 dolls into slit as shown.

Title. Color White die-cut letters with a pencil, glue on Turquoise die-cut letters. Punch 5 Orange ¼" suns, shade Brown and glue on title. Glue title and 2 dolls on page. Add letter stickers.

Photos. Trim photos to fit frames. Glue frames on page slipping edge of Turquoise frame under top of sandcastle. Glue a doll to each frame.

Toys, toys, toys… from background paper to action pull-ups, toys are the theme of these happy pages.

Playtime

MATERIALS: Design Originals 12" paper (2 #0407 *Toys of Yesteryear, Yellow Plaid*) • 12" Cardstock (2 Peach, Black, White, Gray, Yellow, Burgundy, Pink, Blue, Tan, Green) • Punches (1/8", 3/16" 1/4", 5/16", 5/8", 1", 1 1/2" and 2" Circle; 1 1/2", 1 7/8", 2" and 2 1/4" Oval; 2" Star; 1 1/4" Square; 1 3/4" Building Block; 1 1/8" Smiley; 1/4" Moon; 1 3/4" Doll; Ducks Corner) • 1 1/4" letter template • Letter stickers (3/8" Black) • Gel pens (Gold, Brown, Black, Burgundy, Green) • Chalk (Blue, Gray, Brown, Burgundy, Green) • Wavy edge scissors • 2 paper brads • 1/2" wiggle eye

INSTRUCTIONS:

Page. Trim Peach cardstock to fit and glue on album pages. Trim Toys of Yesteryear sheets and glue on Peach cardstock.

Title. Cut or punch 8 Burgundy building blocks and 8 Pink 1 1/4" squares. Shade edges with Burgundy chalk. Cut Yellow and Blue letters, trim slightly. Shade Yellow letters with Brown chalk and outline with Gold. Glue on Pink squares. Glue title on page referring to photo. Outline with Black.

Box Frame. Cut 4 3/8" x 4 1/2" Pink cardstock for box front and lid. Use pattern to cut Blue and Pink box sides and Pink alphabet block. Cut Yellow and Burgundy letters. Shade Yellow letter with Brown chalk and outline with Brown pen. Arrange box on page and glue leaving top of box front open. Cut 4" Burgundy square and 3 3/4" White square trimmed with deckle scissors. Glue White square on Burgundy and add trimmed photo. Punch shapes for Jack, cut and glue together referring to photos. Glue Jack on back of 4" Burgundy square. Shade and outline with matching colors. Cut 3" x 3 1/2" Burgundy and 2 3/4" x 3 1/4" White rectangles. Punch Burgundy with ducks corner. Glue scraps of Yellow on back of ducks and ducks on box. Insert White rectangle in corners and add journaling and letter stickers. Place photo in pocket.

Horse Frame. Use patterns to cut cardstock head, ears, body, tail and legs for horse. Referring to photo, punch 1 1/2", 1 7/8" and 2" ovals for neck, 3/4" circles for tail, 5/8" circle for eye, 1" circle for pommel and 1 1/2" circles for hooves. Trim if needed. Shade and outline all horse shapes. Place 2 legs under body and 2 legs on top of body. Punch holes through legs and body and insert brads. Flatten brad backs. Glue saddle, horse body pieces and eye pieces on page. Test leg movement.

Cut 2 saddles from White cardstock. Cut Pink saddle with hinge. Fold hinge down. Cut saddle blanket from Plaid paper and girth from Yellow cardstock. Cut 'Lift' sign from Burgundy and Yellow cardstock. Glue on saddle blanket. Trim photo to fit inside saddle. Cut journaling sign from Green and White cardstock. Glue inside saddle and add journaling. Glue hinge behind photo piece. Glue girth and saddle on body.

ALPHABET BLOCK 1 1/4" X 2"

BOX RIGHT SIDE 1 1/2" X 5 1/2"

BOX LID 4 1/2" X 4 3/8"

BOX LEFT SIDE 1 1/2" X 5 1/2"

BOX FRONT 4 1/2" X 4 3/8"

How to Make Pull-Up Pockets

Page Preparation. Prepare page with cardstock or background paper. Choose design elements and plan placement of photos and position of pocket to hold pull-up.

Frame. A pull-up frame is a pocket used to display a photo. The photo can be visible above the pocket or hidden inside the pocket. For hidden photos, a cardstock shape is glued to back of photo and the shape is pulled from the pocket. Use patterns, templates or die cuts for pocket and pull-up shapes. Trace on cardstock or background paper glued on cardstock. Cut out. Glue sides and bottom of pocket on page. Crop photo and glue on bottom of pull-up shape. Place photo in pocket.

Finish. Crop and mat additional photos. Glue remaining design elements and photos on page. Title page and add journaling.

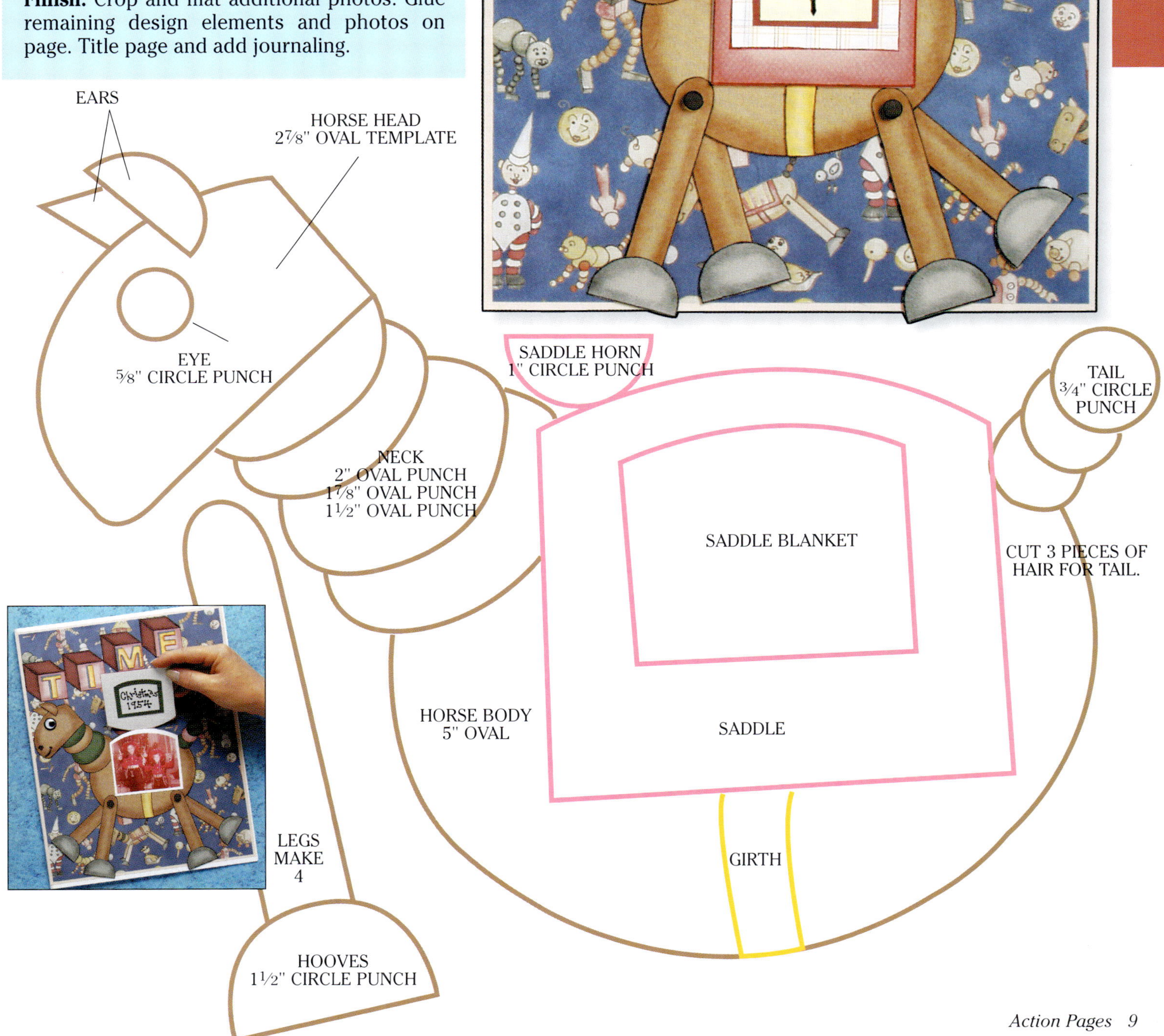

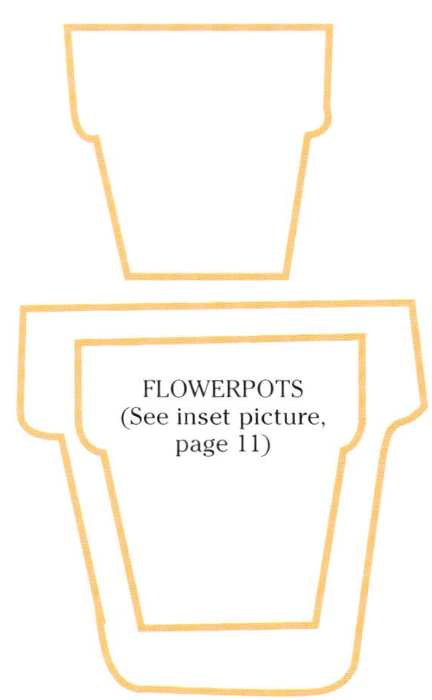

Patchwork Quilter

MATERIALS: Design Originals 12" paper (*#0413 Heritage Quilt, Red Print, Yellow Print, Blue Print*) • 12" Cardstock (White, Black, Gray, Red, Blue, Dual Tone Yellow) • Letter stickers ($\frac{3}{4}$" Black, Yellow, Red, Blue, $\frac{3}{8}$" Black) • Journaling sticker • Punches ($\frac{1}{4}$", $\frac{3}{8}$", $\frac{5}{8}$", $\frac{3}{4}$", 1" and $1\frac{1}{4}$" Square; $1\frac{1}{4}$" and $1\frac{3}{4}$" Building Block; $\frac{1}{8}$", $\frac{3}{16}$", $\frac{1}{4}$", $\frac{5}{16}$" and $\frac{1}{2}$" Circle; $\frac{3}{16}$" and $\frac{5}{8}$" Heart; $\frac{1}{2}$" Primitive Heart; $\frac{5}{16}$" Diamond; $\frac{1}{2}$" Oval; $\frac{5}{8}$" Six Point Star) • $1\frac{7}{8}$" square template • Black Gel pen

INSTRUCTIONS:

Page. Trim paper to fit and glue on album page. Cut $7\frac{1}{2}$" x $7\frac{3}{4}$" Red, 7" x $7\frac{1}{4}$" Blue, $6\frac{1}{2}$" x $7\frac{1}{4}$" Yellow and $6\frac{1}{2}$" x $6\frac{3}{4}$" Yellow pieces of cardstock.

Open the quilt block to discover a photo of a loved one and journaling wisdom inside.

Frame. Score and make a vertical fold $\frac{1}{2}$" from the edge of larger Yellow cardstock. Measure and mark center. Cut diagonal window using template. Glue Yellow cardstock pieces together to make door. Glue door on Red and Blue cardstock pieces. Glue to page.

Quilt Block. Cut $2\frac{3}{4}$" Yellow square and cut opening using template. Glue on front of door opening. Punch 4 each Red and Yellow Print large building blocks, 4 Blue Print small building blocks and 4 Red cardstock small building blocks. Glue pieces into quilt block referring to photo. Punch 4 Blue stars, glue in place.

Photo. Crop and mount photo on 4" x $4\frac{1}{2}$" Blue and $4\frac{1}{2}$" x 5" Red cardstock. Apply Black letter stickers above photo. Cut $2\frac{3}{4}$" Red square and cut opening using template. Glue on back of door opening. Cut $1\frac{1}{4}$" x $2\frac{1}{4}$" Blue and $1\frac{1}{8}$" x $2\frac{1}{8}$" White cardstock. Glue together and apply journaling sticker. Glue below opening.

For scissors, punch primitive heart and two $\frac{1}{2}$" circles from Gray cardstock. Punch $\frac{3}{8}$" circles to make handles. Punch $\frac{3}{16}$" Black and $\frac{1}{8}$" White circles for hinge. Punch $\frac{1}{2}$" Gray cardstock ovals and $\frac{5}{8}$" Yellow square for spool. Glue spool and scissors on photo frame. Add details with Black pen.

Title & Borders. Punch assorted color squares (eight $\frac{1}{4}$", eight $\frac{3}{8}$", seven $\frac{5}{8}$", seven $\frac{3}{4}$", sixteen 1" and nine $1\frac{1}{4}$"). Punch assorted shapes (seven $\frac{1}{4}$" circles, two $\frac{1}{2}$" circles, two $\frac{3}{8}$" stars, four $\frac{3}{16}$" hearts, three $\frac{5}{8}$" hearts, twelve $\frac{5}{16}$" diamonds). Glue punched shapes as shown. Apply large letter stickers. Cut $1\frac{3}{4}$" x $9\frac{1}{2}$" and 1" x $9\frac{1}{2}$" Yellow, $1\frac{1}{8}$" x $9\frac{1}{2}$" and $2\frac{1}{8}$" x $9\frac{1}{2}$" Blue and two $\frac{1}{2}$" x $9\frac{1}{2}$" Red strips. Trim Red strips with zig zag scissors. Glue strips together and on page as shown. Glue punch art to page. Draw stitch marks with gel pen.

To Our Home

Lift-Up Flap

Welcome to Our Home

MATERIALS: Design Originals 12" papers (*#0424 Home Style Bricks, #0422 Beach & Sunny Sky, #0423 Clouds in the Sky, #0420 Deep in the Forest, Pink Print*) • 12" Cardstock (White, Green, Pink, Hot Pink, Gold, Light Brown, Brown, Burgundy, Peach) • Punches (1/8", 3/16" and 5/16" Circle; 1/4", 5/8", 1" and 1 1/4" Flower; 7/8" Flower #1 and Flower #2; 3/8" and 5/8" Birch Leaf; 7/8" Rectangle; 5/8" Daisy; 1 3/8" Flowerpot; 5/8" Grapes; 7/8" Dusty Miller Leaf; 1 1/4" Fern; 2 3/16" Elongated Oval; Crown Border; Fancy Feather Border; Swirl #4 Border; Corner Rounder) • Letter stickers (3/8" Yellow) • Gel pens (Black, Brown, Burgundy) • Chalk (Burgundy, Gray, Pink, Brown, Blue) • Wavy edge scissors

INSTRUCTIONS:

Page. Trim Green cardstock to fit and glue on album page. Trim *Home Style Bricks* to fit and glue on page. Trim Green cardstock to 7 1/2" x 9 1/2" and glue to page as shown.

Title. From *Beach and Sky* papers, punch ferns, 7/8" flowers and 3/16" circles. Punch a White elongated oval. Punch a Brown swirl border. Glue border pieces to oval and write 'Welcome' with Burgundy pen. Shade edge with Blue chalk and pen-stitch with Burgundy and Black pens. Glue swag and oval referring to photo.

Door. Cut 7 3/4" x 9 1/4" Light Brown cardstock piece. Score 1/2" from edge and fold for hinge. Cut 7 1/4" x 9 1/4" Light Brown and White cardstock. Glue Light Brown cardstock on hinge. Close door and glue White cardstock on front. Draw door panels with Black pen and shade with Pink, Burgundy and Gray chalk. Punch 7/8" rectangle and 5/16" circle from Gold cardstock. Outline with Black and Brown pens and shade Gray. Glue on door for knob. Glue door on Green cardstock.

For wreath, punch Brown cardstock dusty miller leaves and swirls and Green cardstock feathers. From *Beach and Sky* papers, punch 5/8" flowers, 5/8" grapes, 3/8" birch leaves and 3/16" circles. Glue on door.

Photos. Round corners of photos. Cut mats from *Home Style Bricks* and cardstock. Trim with wavy edge scissors. Glue mats and photos inside door.

From *Beach and Sky*, print paper and Burgundy cardstock, punch 1/4", 5/8", 7/8", 1" and 1 1/4" flowers, 5/8" birch leaves and 1/8" circles. Layer and glue on photo corners.

Journaling. Punch 2 flowerpots from Peach cardstock. Trim one to a smaller size. Use pattern to cut third pot. Outline with Brown pen and shade with Brown chalk. Punch dusty miller leaves from *Forest* paper. Punch 3 Brown 7/8" rectangles and trim for trunks. Glue trunks and leaves on page and flowerpots over trunks. Apply letter stickers and date.

Open the door to memories. Pots with flowers and a wreath bloom with the love you find at home.

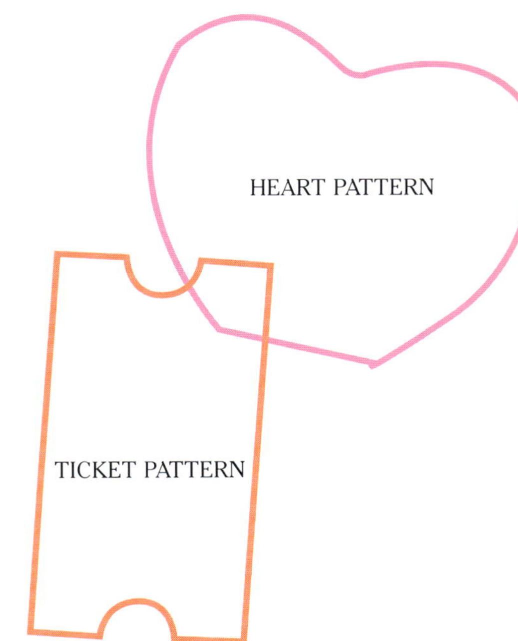

Musical

MATERIALS: Design Originals 12" paper (*#0406 Music Melody*) • Sparkle paper (Red, White, Black) • 12" Cardstock (2 Black, White, Red, Pink) • Punches (1/8" and 5/16" Circle; 1 1/8" and 1 1/4" Oval; 1 1/4" Scallop Oval; 2" Heart; 2" Scallop Heart; 1/2" Primitive Heart; 7/8" and 1 1/2" Rectangle; Music Border) • 1 1/4" letter template or 1 1/4" letter punches • Letter stickers (3/8" Black) • Gel pens (Black, Red, Yellow, Pink) • Chalk (Gray) • Pop dots • Wavy edge scissors • 6" of 1/8" Red satin ribbon • Small Red and Pink ribbon roses

INSTRUCTIONS:

Page. Trim Black cardstock to fit and glue on page. Cut an 8" wide *Music Melody* paper strip and glue on page. Cut a 1/2" wide Red cardstock strip, trim with wavy edge scissors. Glue in place.

Title. Cut or punch letters from *Music Melody* paper and glue down the edge of page.

Photo. Cut 5" x 6" Black cardstock, 4 1/2" x 5 1/2" *Music Melody* paper, 4 1/4" x 5 1/4" Red Sparkle paper and Black cardstock for mats. Punch music notes around edge of Red Sparkle. Layer and glue mats and photo on page.

Doors. Cut 2 White 2" x 4 1/2" cardstock pieces. Score and make fold on each piece to make 2" x 2 1/4" door frames.

For shirt, draw vertical line down center of one frame. Punch 2 White 7/8" rectangles, trim at an angle to make collar. Chalk edges and glue on shirt. Cut 1 3/4" x 2" Black and Red cardstock rectangles. Trim at angles to form Vs. Glue Black on shirt for jacket and Red for cummerbund. Draw Black and White lines with pens. Punch 1/8" Black Sparkle circles, glue on shirt for buttons. Punch Red Sparkle primitive heart. Glue heart on jacket and Red rose on heart. Tie bow, trim ends and glue on collar.

For dress, cut and glue 2" x 2 1/4" Peach piece on front of second frame. Punch 2 Pink 7/8" rectangles, Gray scallop oval, Pink heart and White scallop heart. Add pen details and shade with chalk. Glue dress on frame. Trim bottom of frame around heart and cut off excess oval. Punch 9 White Sparkle 1/8" circles. Glue around neck for necklace. Glue Pink rose in place.

Punch Red and Pink 1 1/4" ovals for mats. Punch photos with 1 1/8" oval punch, glue on mats. Glue mats in frame and add letter stickers and Black music notes.

Journaling. Punch 1 1/2" Red and White rectangles. Trim White rectangles. Punch ends of rectangles with 5/16" circle punch. Glue together. Write words and draw cat face with pens. Cut 1" x 2 1/4" Black and 7/8" x 2 1/8" White cardstock rectangles. Trim White with wavy edge scissors. Write words with pen and glue on Black rectangle. Glue tickets and journaling as shown.

Hit a high note when you make a page filled with remembrances of a night at the musical theater.

Make quick and easy Holiday cards!

1st Christmas Page & Christmas Cards

MATERIALS: Design Originals 12" paper (*#0410 Seasonal Postcards*) • Red mulberry paper • 12" Cardstock (Green, Light Green, Red, Ivory, White) • Punches (3⁄16" and 1⁄4" Circle; 5⁄8", 1" and 2 7⁄8" Holly Leaf; Arlon Heritage Square Corner) • 3⁄8" and 1" letter templates • Gel pens (Black, Brown, Red, Gold) • Old Photo

INSTRUCTIONS:

Page. Trim Green and Ivory cardstock to fit and glue on album page.

Border. Cut a 3" wide Red cardstock strip. Glue on edge of page. Cut 6 *Postcards* and glue on strip.

Door. Photocopy an old photo enlarging or reducing as needed. Cut out. Cut 3 3⁄4" x 9 1⁄2" Red cardstock, score and fold in center. Cut 2 Green 3 1⁄2" x 4 1⁄2" and one White 3 3⁄4" x 4 1⁄2" cardstock pieces. Glue Green to front and inside of card. Glue White to back of card front. Glue photocopies on frame. Glue frame to page.

Cut 2 1⁄2" x 3 1⁄2" Light Green and 2 1⁄4" x 3 1⁄4" Ivory cardstock. Punch corners of Ivory. Cut 2 3⁄4" x 3 3⁄4" Red mulberry paper. Pull edges with fingers to fray. Layer and glue. Punch 2 Green 5⁄8" holly leaves and 3 Red 3⁄16" circles. Glue as shown. Journal with Black pen.

Finish. Cut 1 1⁄8" x 3 1⁄8" Green and 1" x 3" Ivory rectangles. Layer and glue on page. Journal with Black and Brown pens.

Make title using templates and Gold, Red and Black pens.

Punch 6 Light Green 1", 6 Green 2 7⁄8" holly leaves and 10 Red 3⁄8" circles. Glue as shown.

Cards - Cut out a postcard, trim edges with wavy scissors. Cut a piece of cardstock 4" x 9". Fold in half then glue a postcard to the front. Mount on a second piece of cardstock in the color of your choice and use small letter stickers to write a greeting. Trim edges as desired.

A child's Christmas from long ago is showcased on a page filled with vintage charm and delicate colorful cards.

Lift-Up Flap

Place on fold.

Place on fold.

CHINESE LANTERN PATTERN

Open the lantern to discover the mystery and color of the Orient. Enhance the page with Asian themed papers and rubber stamp art.

Trip to the Orient

MATERIALS: Design Originals 12" paper (*#0417 Floral on Green, #0393 Feng Shui*) • 12" Cardstock (White, 2 Black, Tan, Brown, Light Green, Green, Burgundy, Blue, Yellow) • Punches ($\frac{1}{4}$", $\frac{5}{16}$" and $\frac{1}{2}$" Circle; 1" and $1\frac{1}{4}$" Oval; $\frac{3}{8}$" Birch Leaf; $1\frac{7}{8}$" Bare Tree; 1" Dove; Hanover Heritage Square Corner) • $\frac{3}{8}$" letter template • Letter stickers ($\frac{3}{4}$" Red) • Chinese lantern rubber stamp • Black ink pad • Gel pens (Black, Green) • Chalk (Green, Gray) • Colored pencils

INSTRUCTIONS:

Page. Trim Black cardstock to fit and glue on album page. Trim Light Green cardstock and *Floral on Green* paper to fit and glue on page.

Title. Cut Burgundy $3\frac{3}{8}$" x $8\frac{7}{8}$", Dark Green $3\frac{1}{8}$" x $8\frac{5}{8}$" and Tan $2\frac{7}{8}$" x $8\frac{3}{8}$" pieces. Layer and glue on top of page. Stamp lanterns on White cardstock, cut out. Color with pencils and apply letter stickers. Glue lanterns and finish title with letter template and Green and Black pens.

Door. Cut Burgundy $6\frac{1}{4}$" x 8" cardstock and *Feng Shui* $6\frac{1}{8}$" x $7\frac{7}{8}$" paper pieces. Glue on page. For handle, punch Black 1" oval and repunch with $1\frac{1}{4}$" oval. For loop on bottom, punch Black $\frac{1}{4}$" circle and repunch with $\frac{5}{16}$" circle. Cut 2 Green and one White lantern using pattern. Glue one Green and White lanterns together. Glue handle, loop and remaining Green lantern on page. Score and fold top of glued lanterns, glue fold to lantern on page.

On White lantern, draw details with pen, color with pencils and shade with chalk. Punch Brown bare trees to make branches. Add Green birch leaves. Punch $\frac{1}{2}$" Yellow circles for fruit and Blue doves. Shade with chalk and add details with Black pen. Glue to lantern.

Photo. Use oval template to crop photo and make cardstock mats. Cut Burgundy $1\frac{3}{8}$" x $2\frac{3}{4}$" and White $1\frac{1}{8}$" x $2\frac{1}{2}$"rectangles. Punch corners in White rectangle. Layer and glue mats, photo and journaling rectangles inside lantern. Write journaling with Black pen.

Family Affair

MATERIALS: Design Originals 12" paper (*#0415 Wallpaper on Sepia, #0416 Diamonds on Ivory, Gold Print*) • 12" Cardstock (White, Rust, Burgundy, Gold, Dark Gray, Mauve) • Punches (1/8", 5/16", 1/2", 5/8" 1 1/4" and 2" Circle; 2" and 2 1/4" Oval; 1 3/4" and 2" Heart; 1" Bow; 1" Heart Frame; 1" Star Frame; 1" Fleur de Lis Frame; Crown Border; Victoria Corner) • Templates (1 3/4", 2" and 3 1/8" Circle, 1 3/4", 2" and 3 1/8" Heart, 2", 2 1/4" and 3 3/8" Oval) • Letter stickers (1/2" and 5/8" Burgundy) • Gel pen (Black) • Markers (Light Brown, Burgundy, Black) • Chalk (Brown, Burgundy) • 3 paper brads

INSTRUCTIONS:

Page. Trim *Wallpaper* paper to fit and glue on album page. Cut 2 1/4" wide strips of Gold cardstock, glue on top and bottom of page.

Photos. Cut a large circle, an oval and a heart from Gold cardstock and Gold Print. Glue cardstock shapes on page. Crop photos using templates and glue on Gold shapes. Punch or cut medium shapes from Dark Gray and small shapes from *Diamonds on Ivory* using templates. Glue on Gold print shapes. Punch 1/8" holes through Gold Print shapes and page. Insert brads, spread ends to secure. Glue White cardstock to back of page. Glue 5/16" Gold Print circles on brads. Punch Gold frames and glue on shapes.

Journaling. Cut 1 1/2" x 2 1/2" and 2 1/8" x 2 3/4" Gold, 1 1/4" x 2 1/4" and 2" x 2 5/8" Burgundy and 1 1/8" x 2 3/8" and 1 7/8" x 2 1/2" *Diamonds on Ivory* rectangles. Corner punch *Diamonds on Ivory* rectangles. Glue rectangles together and on page. Apply stickers.

Cut swag from *Diamonds on Ivory*, embellish with markers and glue on page. Apply letter stickers. Punch 1/2" Gold Print and 5/8" Burgundy circles. Glue on swag. Punch 3 Gold crown borders and 3 Mauve bows. Cut two 1" and one 2" Mauve 1/4" strips. Shade with chalk and markers. Glue bows and strips above shapes for hangers. Trim borders. Glue to swag and rectangles.

Victorian style papers in rich Burgundy and Gold highlight the splendor of a military ball.

How to Make an Open-Door Frame

Page Preparation. There are many ways to make Open-Door Frames. Choose door size and direction of motion. Doors can open on one side like a book or lift up like a tablet. They can fold up accordion style or open in the center. Cutting a window in the door to display photos is another option. For simple doors, prepare album page with background paper and plan page design.

Doors. Use standard piece of cardstock to cut rectangle. Cover with decorative paper if desired. Turn cardstock over and score horizontal line down center. Fold on line. Use template to cut hole in door.

Generations

MATERIALS: Design Originals 12" paper (*#0419 Corners on Brown, Flower Border from papers book #3326*) • 12" Cardstock (3 Eggplant, Mauve, Light Brown, Dark Brown, Rust) • Punches (Hanover Heritage Square Corner; Deco Corner Lacing; Corner Rounder) • Circle template • Letter stickers ($\frac{1}{4}$" Black, $\frac{7}{8}$" Beige print)

INSTRUCTIONS:

Page. Trim one Eggplant cardstock to $10\frac{1}{2}$". Use a ruler and pencil to mark the center of opening. Cut a 5" circle.

Frame. Glue *Corners on Brown* to second piece of Eggplant cardstock. Cut out floral images from *Corners on Brown*. Layer and glue around opening. Apply Beige letter stickers. Cut page in half vertically with craft knife. Measure $\frac{1}{2}$" from end of each half, score and fold. Trim third piece of Eggplant cardstock to $9\frac{1}{2}$" and glue on scored edges to hold photo. Punch corners of Dark Brown cardstock. Cut off corners and glue on Rust cardstock. Cut again and glue to outer corners of doors.

Photo & Journaling. Crop and mount photo on cardstock and *Flower Border* paper. Position photo under opening, mark and glue on page. Trim overlapping floral images. Cut squares of *Flower Border* paper and $2\frac{1}{8}$" Mauve and $2\frac{3}{8}$" Dark Brown cardstock squares. Punch *Flower Border* paper with corner rounder and Mauve with deco corner. Glue squares together. Apply Black letter stickers and glue under photo.

Finish. Glue on album page.

A cherished photo of a generation past is elegantly framed and viewed through an open door surrounded by a blooming wreath.

Photos. Crop and mat photos. Glue inside or on door. Add stickers or punch art and journaling that will show when the door is opened.

Page Assembly. Glue door frame on page. Glue additional photos and design elements on page. Add title.

Folded Hinges. If door is larger than folded cardstock, use 2 pieces of cardstock connected with a creased hinge. Cut one piece ½" larger on one side than the other. Fold and score larger cardstock ½" from edge. Apply glue or photo tape inside fold and insert smaller cardstock. Press firmly. Use hinged door frames to cover entire album page or glue individual doors on page.

Open-Doors Frame

Autumn Leaves

MATERIALS: Design Originals 12" paper (*#0425 Fall Acorns & Leaves*) • 12" Cardstock (White, Tan, Brown, Rust, Red, Burgundy, Green, Violet, Lavender, Yellow) • Letter stickers (⅜" multi color) • Punches (1¼" and 1½" Scallop Square; Filmstrip Border; ½" Dusty Miller Leaf; ¾" and 1" Maple Leaf; Oak Leaf; White Oak Leaf; Hawthorn Leaf; ⅛" Circle) • 3⅜" oval template • Gel pens (Brown, Black, Red) • Multi color raffia

INSTRUCTIONS:

Page. Cut Brown cardstock to fit and glue on album page. Cut *Fall Acorns & Leaves* paper to fit and glue on page.

Title. Cut ⅞" x 2" Brown and ¾" x 1⅞" White rectangles. Glue together and write a title with Black and Brown pens. Glue on page. Punch 6 each of 1" Rust maple leaves, 1¼" Brown and 1½" Tan scallop squares. Glue together and arrange across page overlapping corners. Apply letter stickers.

Frame. Cut 7¾" x 12" piece of Tan cardstock. Measure and mark 2 horizontal lines 3" from each end. Score and fold creating door. Erase lines. Cut opening using oval template. Punch leaves referring to photo. Glue dusty miller leaves around opening. Overlap and glue assorted leaves over dusty miller leaves. Draw veins with Brown pen. Punch 2 holes, thread raffia through holes and tie bow. Trim.

Photo & Journaling. Crop and mat photo on Red cardstock. Punch Tan cardstock with filmstrip border, collect pieces and glue around edge of photo. Mark position of photo and glue under opening. Write name and age with Black and Red gel pens.

This charming page features the same photo inside and out. You'll love the clever Punch Art autumn leaves title.

Tip - Substitute animal stickers for punch art animals. Attach stickers to cardstock, cut out and glue on ark.

Punch cardstock and paper as follows:

Doves & Nest.
2 White - 1/2" Circles, 4 White - 3/8" Birch Leaves
2 Yellow - 3/16 " Diamonds
Brown - 1 7/8" Oval, 2 Tan - 1 1/2" Suns

Hearts on Ark.
Red - 1 1/8", Black - 1 1/4" Heart

Portholes.
3 Gold - 1/2", 3 Black - 5/8" Circle

Giraffes.
4 Tan - 1/8" Circles, 4 Brown - 1/4" Rectangles
2 Animal Print -7/8", 2 Animal Print -1 1/8" Footprints
4 Animal Print - 3/8" Birch Leaves
4 Animal Print - Grass Borders

Noah.
Pink - 1 3/4" Doll
Stripe - 1 1/8" and Blue 1 1/4" Hearts
Red - 1/2" and Red 7/8" Rectangles
Gray - 5/8" Birch Leaf, Brown - hand cut staff

Lions.
2 Peach and 2 Orange - 1 1/2" Suns
4 Green - 3/16", 8 Tan - 5/16", 2 Tan - 3/4" Circles
2 Black 5/8" Pawprints

Zebras.
2 White - 1/8" Circles, 2 Black - Grass Borders
4 Animal Print - 3/8" Birch Leaves
2 Animal Print - 7/8", 2 Animal Print - 1 1/8" Footprints

Elephants.
Red - 1/4", Gray - 1 1/4", 2 Gray - 1 1/2" Hearts

Waves.
8 White - 1 1/4" and 8 Blue - 1 1/2" Swirl

Baby for Journaling Heart.
Blue - 1/8", Pink - 3/16", Peach - 1/2" Circles,
Brown - 1/2" Swirl, Blue - 3/8" Heart

Continue the theme of a baby shower with an ark full of punch art animals that pop to life. Rain shower paper provides the perfect background.

Shower of Love

MATERIALS: Design Originals 12" paper (2 #0423 *Clouds in the Sky*, Multi Color Stripe, Animal Print) • 12" Cardstock (Black, White, Yellow, Red, Gold, Orange, Brown, Green, Gray, Blue, Pink, Peach) • Punches (1 3/4" Doll; 1" Romper; 1/8", 3/16", 5/16", 1/2", 5/8", 3/4", 2" Circle; 1/4", 3/8", 1/2", 5/8", 1 1/8", 1 1/4", 1 1/2" and 1 3/4" Heart; 1 3/4" and 2" Scallop Heart; 1/4", 1/2", 5/8", 1 1/4" and 1 1/2" Swirl; 1/4", 1/2" and 7/8" Rectangle; 3/8", 1/2" and 5/8" Birch Leaf; 1 1/4" Square; 3/16" Diamond; 5/8" Pawprint; 7/8" and 1 1/8" Footprint; 1 1/2" Sun; Grass Border) • Circle template • 1 1/4" letter template • Letter stickers (1/4" Black) • Yellow and Red die-cut frames • Gel pens (Black, Pink, Blue) • Markers (Brown, Blue, Green, Gray, Red) • Chalk (Pink, Gray, Brown)

INSTRUCTIONS:

Page. Trim 2 *Clouds in the Sky* to fit and glue on album pages. Cut 7/8" wide strips of Blue cardstock. Punch with 5/8" swirls. Cut away paper above swirls to make the wave border. Outline with a Black pen and shade with Blue chalk. Glue on the bottom of pages. Punch Red 1 3/4" and 2" scallop hearts and Yellow 1 1/2" and 2 3/4"hearts. Glue on page and apply letter stickers.

Title. Punch 1 1/4" Yellow cardstock squares. Trace letters using template on Yellow squares, cut out. Trace on Red cardstock, enlarging slightly. Punch 3/8" and 1/2" hearts in Yellow letters. Outline letters with Black pen and shade with Gray chalk. Glue on clouds as shown. Apply Black stickers to spell 'of'.

Photos. Crop photos to fit frames, glue in frames. Glue frames on page.

Pop-Up. Using pattern, trace and cut ark from White cardstock. Cut slits to accommodate figures. Embellish with pens, markers and chalk. Score and mountain fold edges and center of ark. Crop 1 7/8" photos and cut 2" Black cardstock circles. Glue on ark. Make animals, people and embellishments referring to photo for color and placement. Outline shapes with pens and shade with chalk. Glue shapes on ark and ark on page.

Cruise down memory lane... this nautical page commemorates a happy time and a dear friendship.

Cruisin'

MATERIALS: Design Originals 12" paper (2 #0398 *Water & Swirls*, Red Plaid) • 12" Cardstock (Black, White, Red, Gold, Blue, Light Gray, Gray) • Punches (1/8", 3/16", 1/4", 5/16", 1/2", 5/8" and 1 1/2" Circle; 1 1/4", 1 1/2" and 1 3/4" Oval; 1/2" Triangle) • Circle template • Letter stickers (1/4" Black, 1/4" Red, 5/8" Bon Voyage) • Anchor sticker • Gel pen (Black) • Markers (Black, Blue, Gray, Red, Gold) • Chalk (Gray)

INSTRUCTIONS:

Page. Trim 2 *Water & Swirls* to fit and glue on album pages. Cut 4 Gold 1/4" wide strips, glue on the top and bottom of pages.

Title. Cut Red 2 3/4" x 11" and Red Plaid 2 1/2" x 11" strips. Glue diagonally on page, trim. Trace small ship on White cardstock and cut out. Decorate with markers. Trace small ship on Black cardstock enlarging 1/8", cut out. Glue ships on strips.

Journaling. Cut 1 3/4" x 3 3/4" White cardstock rectangle. Apply Bon Voyage and Red letter stickers.

Page Photos. Use circle template to cut frames from White, Red and Gray cardstock. Outline with pens, decorate with markers and shade with chalk. Crop photos to fit behind frames. Glue frames and photos on page. Decorate portholes with 5/16" Light Gray and Black circles. Make hats and anchors referring to photo for colors and placement.

Pop-Up. Cut ship from cardstock using pattern. Score and mountain fold center and side flaps. Cut notches in flaps. Decorate ship with markers and chalk. Glue on page. Punch Black 1/2" circles and Red 5/8" circles. Glue on ship.

Ship Photos. Use circle template to cut frames from Gold and Black cardstock. Outline with Black pen. Crop photos to fit behind frames. Glue frames and photos on ship. Decorate portholes with 1/8" Light Gray and Black circles. Apply anchor and Black letter stickers.

Punch cardstock and paper as follows:

Captain's Hat.
Red 5/16" Circle
Black 1 1/4", Yellow 1 1/2" and White 1 3/4" Ovals

Anchor.
2 Gold 1/4", Gold 5/16" and Gold 1 1/2" Circles
2 Gold 1/2" Triangles

ARK PATTERN

TUG BOAT PATTERN

cruisin

How to Make Pop-Up Centers

Album. Pop-up centers require a 2 page spread. Post bound or strap bound albums work best. These albums lay flat when opened and hold the pages together in the center.

Page Preparation. Glue cardstock or decorative paper on pages. Glue borders on pages if needed. Choose photos and embellishments. Use pattern or template to cut out folded design or use a die cut. Mark placement of photos, embellishments and position of folded design with a pencil.

Motion. Plan direction of motion. For a sharp fold, score along fold line before folding. To make a valley fold, score on back of shape and fold in. To make a mountain fold, score on front of shape and fold out. Test placement to be sure shape will fold flat and will not protrude when album is closed. Apply glue. Attach one side of shape to each page. Match center fold of shape to center spine of album.

Finish. Crop and mat photos. Glue photos and embellishments on pages. Add title and journaling.

BODY PATTERN

BUTTERFLY WINGS

Butterflies flutter and flit among photos of children at play. Hand tinting black and white photocopies adds a touch of color.

Flutter by Butterfly

MATERIALS: Design Originals 12" paper (2 #0396 *Butterflies on Blue*, #0422 *Beach & Sunny Sky*, Jewel Rainbow, Yellow Stripe) • 12" Cardstock (Black, White, Yellow, Blue, Purple, 4 Green) • Punches (1⁄8" and 1⁄4" Circle; 1⁄2" and 1 5⁄8" Butterfly) • 1 1⁄4" letter template or 1 1⁄4" letter punches • Letter stickers (5⁄16" Yellow, 3⁄16" and 1⁄2" Black) • Gel pens (Black) • Chalk (Pink) • Pop dots

INSTRUCTIONS:

Page. Trim 2 Green cardstock sheets to fit and glue on album pages. Trim 2 *Butterflies on Blue* papers to fit and glue on pages.

Photos. Crop and mat photos as desired. Glue on page. Punch 3 White 1 3⁄4" butterflies. Trace shapes on Yellow and Green cardstock, enlarging 1⁄8" and 1⁄4". Cut out. Shade White butterflies with Pink chalk. Score and make valley folds down centers of butterflies, glue together. Apply 3⁄16"Yellow and Black letter stickers and journal with a Black pen. Attach butterflies to page with pop dots.

Title. Trim a 2 3⁄4" wavy strip of *Jewel Rainbow* paper for title. Glue on page. Cut or punch letters from Yellow and Green cardstock. Punch 3⁄8" butterflies from *Jewel Rainbow* and *Beach & Sunny Sky* paper and 3 Black 1⁄8" cardstock circles. Outline and detail butterflies with Black pen. Apply 1⁄2" Black letter stickers. Glue letters, dots and butterflies on title strip as shown.

Pop-Up. Using patterns, cut hearts for wings from Yellow Stripe paper and Green cardstock. Cut body from Black cardstock. Glue hearts together to make wings. Score and make mountain fold down center of body. Glue body on wings. Score and make valley folds on edges of larger wings. Glue folded edges to pages.

Beloved wedding photos deserve a special setting. Pastel frames and an elaborate wedding cake are excellent accents.

CAKE PATTERN

Cuttin' the Cake

MATERIALS: Design Originals 12" papers (2 *#0414 Roses & Letters, Black Stripe,* Vellum) • 12" Cardstock (Black, White, Gray, Gold, Peach, Pink, Green) • Punches ($1\frac{3}{4}$" Doll; 1" Romper; $\frac{1}{4}$", $\frac{5}{16}$" and $\frac{5}{8}$" Circle; $\frac{3}{16}$", $\frac{3}{8}$" and $\frac{7}{8}$" Birch Leaf; $\frac{3}{8}$", $\frac{5}{8}$" and $1\frac{1}{2}$" Flower; $\frac{1}{2}$" and $\frac{7}{8}$" Rectangle; $1\frac{1}{4}$" Bell; $\frac{1}{4}$" Bow; Fancy Feathers Border; Crown Border) • Letter stickers ($\frac{3}{4}$" Pink, $\frac{1}{4}$" Black) • Scallop Lavender and rectangle Pink die-cut frames • Rubber stamps ($\frac{5}{16}$", $\frac{5}{8}$" and $1\frac{1}{2}$" Rose) • Pink ink pad • Gel pens (Black, Red, Gray, White, Gold, Green) • Chalk (Pink, Gray, Brown)

INSTRUCTIONS:

Page. Trim 2 *Roses & Letters* to fit and glue on album pages.

Pop-Up. Cut cake from White cardstock. Outline with Gray pen and shade with Gray chalk. Cut plate from Gold cardstock. Outline with Gold pen and shade edges with Brown. Glue plate on cake. Score and make mountain fold down center of cake and plate. Score and make valley fold down edges of plate. Glue cake on pages.

Photos. Crop and mount photos in frames. Glue Pink cardstock behind corner openings in scallop frames. Glue frames on page.

Finish. Stamp roses on Pink cardstock and cut out with flower punches. Make 15 small, 6 medium and 4 large flowers. From Green cardstock, punch 30 small, 12 medium and 8 large birch leaves. Detail leaves with Green pen. Glue leaves on back of flowers and flowers as shown. Punch Green fancy feathers border and glue on cake.

For bride and groom, punch shapes, embellish and assemble referring to photo for color and placement.

Apply letter stickers to cake and page.

Tip - For realistic flowers, rubber stamp flowers in a darker shade of ink than cardstock. Center punch over stamp image and punch. For each flower, glue 2 or more punched shapes together, offsetting petals.

Punch cardstock and paper as follows:

Groom
- Peach - $1\frac{3}{4}$" Doll
- Gray - 1" Romper
- Stripe - $\frac{7}{8}$" Rectangles
- Gold - $\frac{5}{8}$" Circle
- Gray - $\frac{1}{4}$" Bow

Bride
- Peach - $1\frac{3}{4}$" Doll
- White - $1\frac{1}{4}$" Bell
- White - $\frac{1}{2}$" Rectangle, Black $\frac{5}{16}$" and $\frac{5}{8}$" Circles
- Pink - $\frac{1}{4}$", Green $\frac{3}{8}$" and White $\frac{5}{8}$" Flower
- Pink - Crown Border

PLATE PATTERN

HEY
DIDDLE DIDDLE

Punch cardstock and paper as follows:

Humpty Dumpty.
Black - 1/2" Ovals
Pink, Blue and Red - 1 1/4" Ovals
White and Pink - 1 13/16" Girls
Black - 5/16" Circle
Red and Blue - 1/2" Rectangle
Yellow - 1/4" Bow

Wall.
Home Style Bricks - 1 1/2" Rectangle

Cow & Moon.
Yellow - 1 1/8" Moon
White - 7/8" Cow
Blue - 1/4" and 3/8" Stars
Pink - 1/8" Heart

Dish & Spoon.
2 Pink - 1/8" Circles
Yellow - 1 1/4" Circle
Blue - 1 1/8" Spoon
Peach - 1 3/16" Girls
Red - 1/8" Heart and 1/4 Bow"

Stick Horse.
2 Tan - 5/8" Footprints
Blue - 1/4" Circle
Red - 5/16" Circle
Yellow - 1/4" Star
Gray - 7/8" Rectangle
4 Black - 1/2" Grass
2 Tan - 3/16" Birch Leaves

Dragonfly.
Green - and Brown - 3/4" Dragonfly

Bear.
Brown - 7/8" Bear

Duck.
Yellow - 7/8" Swan,
Blue - 1/8" and 2 Red - 5/16" Circles
Gray - 7/8" Rectangle
2 Pink - 1/8" Hearts

Wild, Wild West Title.
2 3/16" Tan Elongated Oval

Pig.
Pink - 2 1/4" Oval
Pink - 1/2" and 4 Pink - 7/8" Rectangles
2 Pink - 5/8" Strawberries
Red - 1/4" Heart
Pink - Swirl Border #4

Washtub.
Pink and Blue Vellum -
3/16", 1/4" and 5/16" Circles
Brown and Gray - 2 7/8" Circles
Pink - 1/2" Rectangle
2 Blue and Pink Vellum -
Cloud Cartoon Bubbles

Hey Diddle.
2 Black - Music borders
White - Hand cut music staff

Mini Windows Album

CHILD'S PLAY

An album in an album... what a wonderful way to recall special days in the lives of your favorite children.

Child's Play

MATERIALS: Design Originals 12" paper (*#0409 Nursery Rhymes, #0424 Home Style Bricks, Yellow Print*) • Vellum (Pink, Blue) • 12" Cardstock (Black, White, Pale Green, Moss Green, Red, Pink, Blue, Yellow, Peach, Brown, Tan, Gray, Ivory) • Punches ($\frac{1}{8}$", $\frac{3}{16}$", $\frac{1}{4}$", $\frac{5}{16}$", $\frac{3}{4}$", $1\frac{1}{4}$" and $2\frac{7}{8}$" Circle; $\frac{1}{2}$", $1\frac{1}{4}$", 2" and $2\frac{1}{4}$" Oval; $1\frac{1}{4}$" Square, $\frac{1}{2}$", $\frac{7}{8}$" and $1\frac{1}{2}$" Rectangle; $\frac{7}{8}$" Cow; $\frac{5}{8}$" Footprint; $2\frac{1}{4}$" Scallop Oval; $\frac{3}{16}$" and $\frac{3}{8}$" Star; $\frac{3}{16}$" Birch Leaf; $2\frac{3}{16}$" Elongated Oval; $1\frac{3}{16}$" Girl; $\frac{1}{8}$" Heart; $\frac{1}{4}$" Bow; $\frac{5}{8}$" Strawberry; $\frac{7}{8}$" Moon; $\frac{7}{8}$" Bear; $\frac{7}{8}$" Swan; $1\frac{1}{8}$" Spoon; $\frac{1}{2}$" Grass; $\frac{3}{4}$" Dragonfly; Cloud Cartoon Bubble; Swirl Border #4; Music Border) • Letter stickers ($\frac{3}{8}$" Red, $\frac{1}{4}$" and 1" Multi Color, $\frac{3}{16}$" Black) • Gel pens (Black, Brown, White, Pink, Red, Orange) • Chalk (Brown, Gray) • 27" of $\frac{1}{2}$" Red sheer ribbon • Stapler • Repositionable adhesive

INSTRUCTIONS:

Page. Trim Moss Green cardstock to fit and glue on album page.

Title. Cut Red $2\frac{1}{8}$" wide and Pale Green $1\frac{3}{4}$" wide cardstock strips. Glue on page. Punch title characters referring to photo for color and placement. Outline with pens and shade with chalk. Glue characters and apply letter stickers.

Border. Cut White $1\frac{1}{2}$" wide and Red $1\frac{3}{4}$" wide cardstock strips. Tear images from *Nursery Rhymes* paper and glue on White strip, trim edges. Glue border on page.

Album. Cut 3 Ivory 11" x $6\frac{1}{2}$" cardstock rectangles. Tear and glue *Nursery Rhymes* images on front of album. Trim $\frac{1}{8}$" from top and one side of remaining pieces for proper fit. Score horizontal fold line down centers of all 3 rectangles. Fold and slip pages in cover to check fit.

Windows. Punch 4 Pale Green $1\frac{1}{4}$" cardstock squares. Apply repositionable adhesive and arrange on outside edge of cover. Trace outline with pencil. Remove shapes. Center upside down punch over guidelines. Punch 4 windows in cover. Tip: Keep punch steady to avoid slipping and press down evenly.

Slip pages into cover. Spread open, exposing fold line. Align edges and staple together on fold line.

Close album. Using windows in cover for a guide, trace outline of 3 windows on page 3. Leaving top space blank, punch 3 windows. Punch 2 windows on page 5 and one window on page 7. Windows should line up when cover is closed. Viewer can see through windows to page 9.

Place Pale Green squares on blank spaces on pages. Align them directly under window openings. Glue punch art under windows. Note: Pages 10 and 11 are non-functional. They can be glued together or used for additional photos and journaling. Crop and mat photos. Glue on pages. Glue punch art to pages. Apply letter stickers.

Finish. Punch Red $2\frac{1}{4}$" scallop oval and White 2" oval. Glue on front of album and apply Red letter stickers. Spread album open in center and use small punch to make 2 holes through pages and cover. Thread ribbon through holes and tie bow. Trim excess ribbon. Glue back of album on scrapbook page.

FLOWERPOT PATTERN

Add a pot full of bright flowers in full bloom to your garden photos for a page bursting with color.

Your little sprouts bloom from seed packets on a leafy background. Ladybugs and tiny flowers add the finishing touches.

Garden Grows

MATERIALS: Design Originals 12" papers (*#0399 Garden Leaves, 3 Yellow Prints, Yellow Plaid, 3 Red Prints*) • 12" Cardstock (Black, White, Red, Gold, Green) • Punches ($\frac{1}{8}$" and $\frac{1}{2}$" Circle; $\frac{1}{2}$" Oval; $\frac{5}{8}$" Swirl; Celebration Border; Grass Border; Flower Corner; Loire Heritage Square Corner) • Letter stickers ($\frac{3}{16}$" Black, $\frac{3}{8}$" Red) • $1\frac{1}{4}$" Red Plaid die-cut letters • Gel pens (Black, Brown, White) • Chalk (Pink, Yellow) • Red and Yellow raffia ribbon

INSTRUCTIONS:

Page. Trim *Garden Leaves* paper to fit and glue on album page.

Borders. Cut $\frac{7}{8}$" wide and 2" wide Red cardstock, $\frac{3}{4}$" wide and $1\frac{7}{8}$" wide Yellow stripe paper strips. Glue on top and bottom of page. Apply letter stickers to top strip and glue die-cuts to bottom strip. Outline die cut letters with Black pen.

Pocket Envelope

$3\frac{1}{2}$" x $6\frac{1}{4}$"

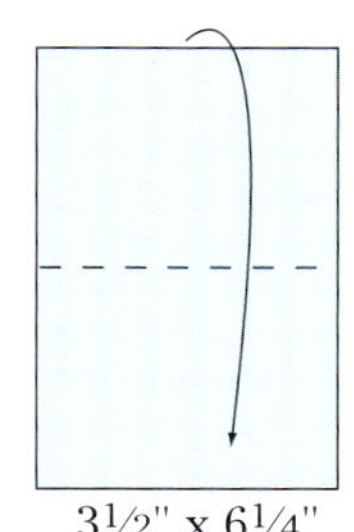

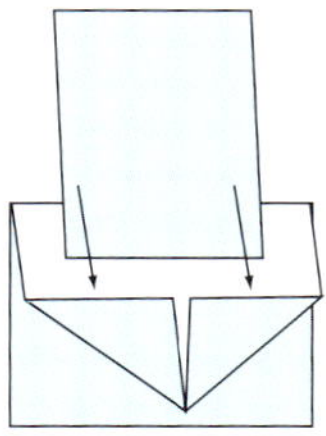

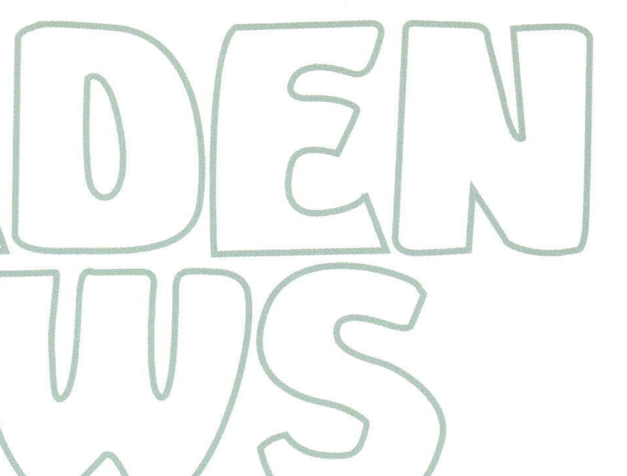

Garden of Color

MATERIALS: Design Originals 12" paper (*#0400 Stepping Stones, #0399 Garden Leaves*) • 12" Cardstock (White, Red, Blue, Lavender, Yellow, Green) • Punches (1⅝" Tulip; 1¼" Flower) • 4½" Red corrugated flowerpot die-cut • Black permanent pen • Deckle edge scissors

INSTRUCTIONS:

Page. Trim *Stepping Stones* paper to fit and glue on album page.

Photos & Title. Cut a 3¾" x 4¼" rectangle and a 3¾" square of Red cardstock. Crop photos and glue on cardstock. Glue on page. Cut 1¾" x 3" White and 2¼" x 3½" Red cardstock rectangles. Glue together and on page. Add title.

Leaves & Flowerpot. Trim *Garden Leaves* around leaf shapes for bottom border. Glue in place. Cut slit in top of flowerpot. Glue edges of flowerpot on page. Cut insert from Red and leaves from Green cardstock. Glue together and write journaling on insert. Punch flowers from Red, Yellow, Blue and Lavender cardstock. Glue on leaves. Place insert in flowerpot.

Garden
of Color

Garden Grows... continued

Pockets. Cut 2 White 3½" x 6¼" cardstock pieces. Score and glue papers on pockets, then fold referring to diagram. Punch ⅛" holes, thread ribbon and tie bows. Punch Green Grass border 4 times. Glue on edge of pockets. Glue down 'V' portions of pockets. Glue pockets on page.

Ladybug. Punch 1 White and 2 Red ½" ovals, 2 Black ⅝" swirls and Black ½" circle. Trim circle and swirls. Assemble ladybug. Draw spots with a White pen and glue ladybugs on pockets.

Frames. Cut 2½" x 3¾" Red and Yellow cardstock rectangles. Cut 2 White 2⅜" x 3⅝" cardstock rectangles. Glue together. Cut White cardstock banners. Outline and write seed names with Black pen. Shade edges with Yellow and Pink chalk. For watermelon, punch Green celebration border and ½" Red oval. Make seeds with Black pen. For flower, punch Green celebration border and Yellow flower corner. Make centers with Brown pen. Glue embellishments on banners. Trim photos. Glue photos and banners on frames. Insert in pockets.

Journaling. Cut 1⅝" x 2½" Red and 1⅜" x 2¼" White rectangles. Punch White with Loire corner. Glue rectangles on page. Punch Green celebrations corner and Yellow flower corner. Glue on White rectangle and make centers with Brown pen. Apply Black letter stickers and date with Black pen.

Outdoor adventures are remembered forever on this page of rugged mountains, bubbling streams and waving grasses.

Outdoors

MATERIALS: Design Originals 12" papers (*#0397 Sky & Clouds, #0400 Stepping Stones, #0398 Water & Swirls, #0399 Garden Leaves*) • Natural corrugated paper • 12" Cardstock (Light Brown) • Letter stickers (¾" rustic) • Gel pen (Black) • Wavy edge scissors

INSTRUCTIONS:

Page. Trim *Sky & Clouds* paper to fit and glue on album page. Cut corrugated and Brown cardstock into rough mountain shapes with wavy scissors. Glue in place. Trim *Stepping Stones* to about 7" tall cutting around the stone shapes. Glue on page. Silhouette cut photos, glue. Trim *Garden Leaves* to about 4½" tall cutting around the leaf shapes on the top and bottom, glue.

Journaling. Write around photos with Black pen. Apply stickers for title.

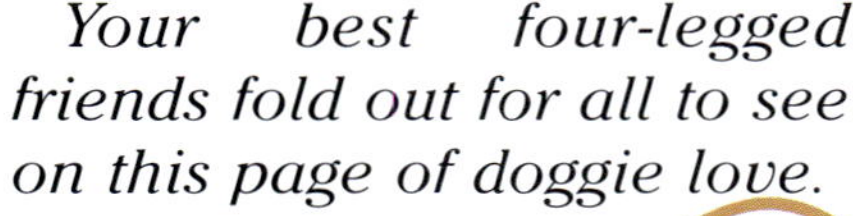

Your best four-legged friends fold out for all to see on this page of doggie love.

Dog Bone

MATERIALS: Design Originals 12" paper *(#0403 Doggone Dog Days)* • Natural corrugated paper • 12" Cardstock (Terra Cotta, Tan) • Letter stickers (¾" rustic)

INSTRUCTIONS:

Page. Trim Tan cardstock to fit and glue on album page. Trim *Doggone Dog Days* to fit and glue on page.

Title. Cut a 3" x 4½" Rust cardstock and a 3½" x 5" corrugated rectangle. Glue together, apply stickers and glue on page.

Accordion Door. Cut a 4" x 12" Rust cardstock and 6½" square of corrugated paper. Glue corrugated paper on page. Score and fold cardstock in thirds. Crop and glue photos on cardstock and cardstock on page. Cut 2 Rust bones and glue on corners.

Hangin' Out

MATERIALS: Design Originals 12" paper *(2 #0397 Sky & Clouds, #0420 Deep in the Forest, Yellow & White Print, Red & White Print, Red Print, Yellow Print, Blue Print, Green Print, White Print)* • Walnut woodgrain paper • 12" Cardstock (White, Black, Brown, Red, Blue, Green, Yellow, Gold, Tan, Peach) • Punches (1¾" Doll; 1" Romper; 1" Dress; 1" Overalls; ¼", ⅝", 1¼" and 2" Circle; ¼", 5/16", ½" and 2¼" Oval; 1¼" Scallop Oval; ¼" and ½" Swirls; ⅛" and ⅜" Heart; ¼" Flower; ⅝" Bear; ⅜" Maple Leaf; ½" Shell; ⅝" Oak Leaf; ⅝" Cloud; ⅝" Bananas; ¼" Bow; ½" Rectangle; Grass Border; Festive Bow Border; Majestic Corner) • 1¼" letter template • Letter stickers (½" Black, ¼" multi color) • Die-cut frames (2 Red 4½" x 5", 2 Yellow 3½" x 4½", 2 Blue 3" square) • Gel pens (Hot Pink, Green, Red, Black, Brown) • Chalk (Brown, Pink, Blue, Red, Yellow, Green, Gray) • Deckle edge scissors •

INSTRUCTIONS:

Pages. Trim *Sky & Cloud* papers and glue on pages.

Clothesline. Trim grass from *Deep in the Forest* paper with deckle scissors. Cut in half and save scraps. Cut ⅜" x 5" strips of Woodgrain paper. Glue strips on pages. Glue grass paper on page. Draw clothesline with a Black pen.

Title. Punch 1¼" Red and Yellow & White circles. Trace letter shapes and trim into puffy letters. Outline letters with Black pen. Shade Yellow letters with Gray chalk and glue letters on page. Complete title with Black stickers. Crop photos and mat with die-cut frames. Glue frames on pages.

Laundry Baskets. Punch 2 Tan 2¼" ovals and trim to shape. Use ½" Tan Ovals punched with ¼" ovals for handles. Draw lines with Brown pens and shade with Brown chalk. Cut 2" slits at top. Punch 2" White circles and trim to fit in openings. Detail with Black pen and shade Gray. Glue circles in baskets. Punch grass borders from *Deep in the Forest* paper. Glue borders and edges of baskets in place.

Clothes on Line. Punch and trim Red and White 1¾" dolls to make long underwear, stocking and shoes. Punch ⅝" bears and ⅜" heart from White and Brown cardstock. Cut heart in half for rabbit ears. Punch Brown Festive Bow border for clothespins. Embellish pieces with gel pens. Shade with chalk referring to photo. Glue shapes to clothesline and clothespins over line.

Children. Punch 1¾" dolls from Peach and Brown cardstock. Cut dolls apart and glue pieces to clothes to make taller, shorter, or appear to move. Trim punched dress to make shirt and overalls to make shorts. Trim scallop oval to make ruffled collar. Cut ⅝" circle in half for shoes. Add ⅜" oval to make cap. Punch majestic corners and trim to create sunbonnet or straw hat. Use punches to make hair. Make bows, buttons and features with mini punches. Add details with gel pens and shade with chalk. Place 2 dolls in baskets. Pull up to make them pop out. Glue remaining dolls to pages.(Refer to book #3320 **Hello Dolly** for more Dolls and clothing ideas.)

Signs. Trim 1½" White and Brown rectangles for signs and handles. Glue pieces together. Apply ¼" letter stickers. Glue signs to dolls' hands.

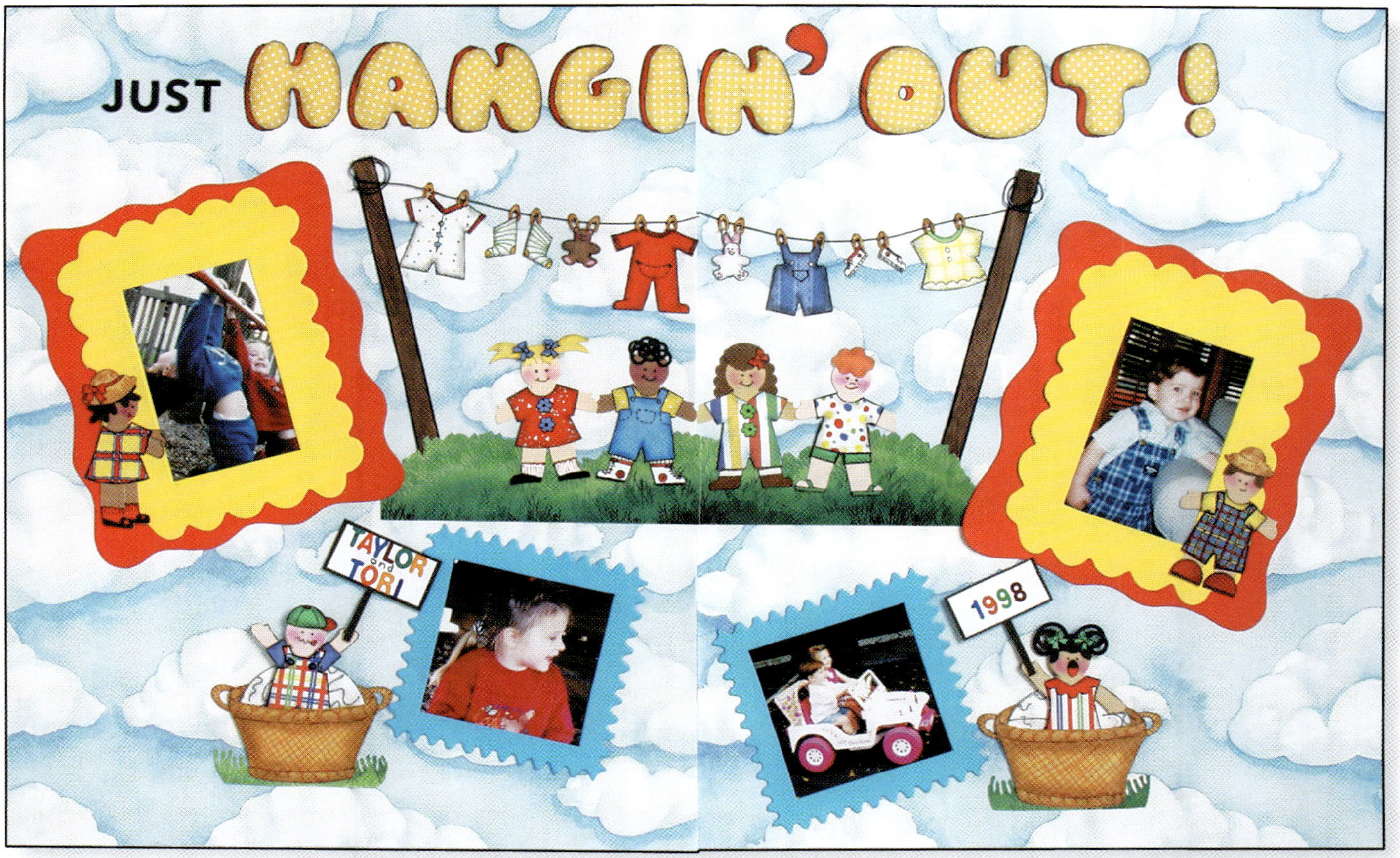

JUST HANGIN' OUT!
TAYLOR and TORI
1998

A line full of clothes, a gang of kids and photos of playtime fun make a page filled to the brim with energy.

BASKET PATTERN

JUST HANGIN' OUT!
1998

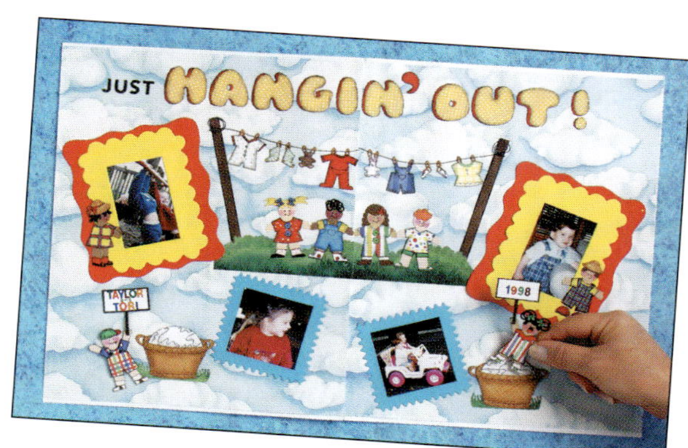

Pull dolls and signs out of baskets to create fun and interest on the page.

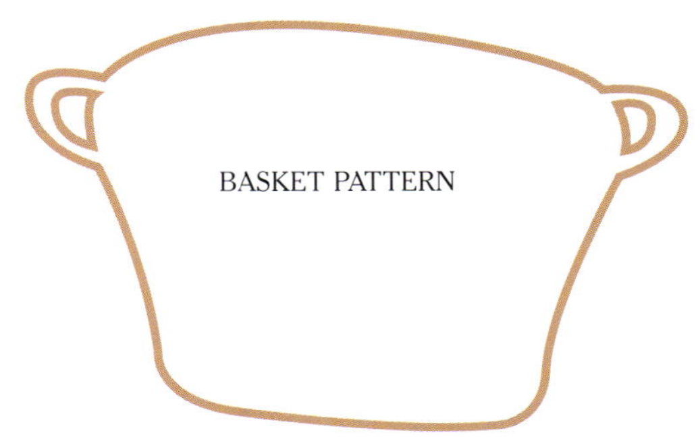

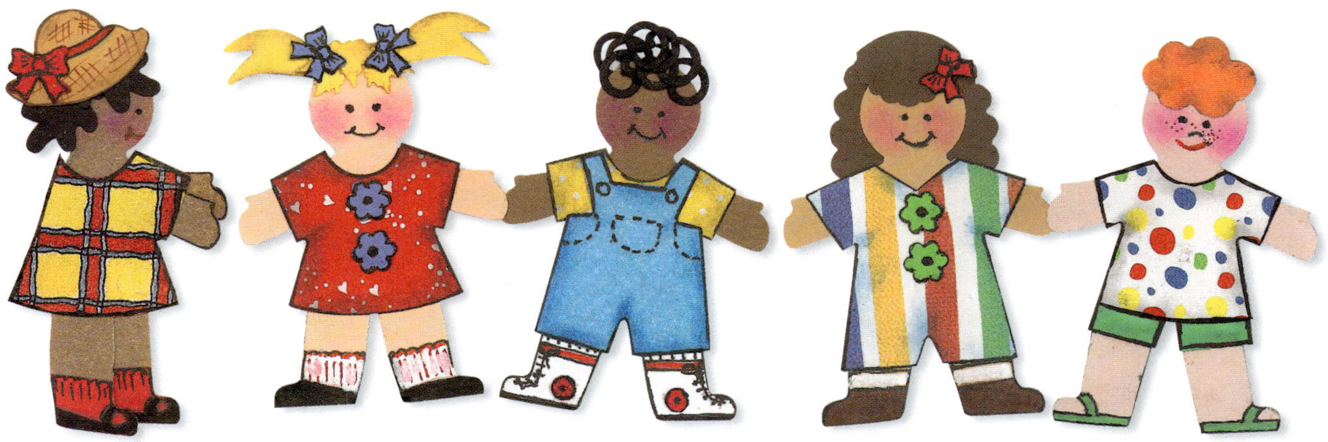

Pocket Pull-Ups

Little, pastel buntings are the perfect pockets for silhouette photos of tiny babies. Punch art toys add to the theme.

Cut Here

BUNTING PATTERN

Baby Love

MATERIALS: Design Originals 12" paper (*#0402 Little Baby Faces*) • 12" Cardstock (Black, White, Yellow, Pink, Green, Peach, Lavender, Purple) • Punches (1/8", 3/16", 5/16", 5/8", 3/4" and 1 1/4" Circle; 3/4" and 2 1/4" Heart; 5/8" Scallop Heart; 1/4" Country Heart; 1/4" Flower; 1/4" and 7/8" Bow; 1/2" and 1 1/2" Rectangle; 1" Smiley; 1/4" Swirl; 5/8" Footprint; Swirl Border #4; Duck Corner) • 1 1/4" letter template • Letter stickers (1/4" Black) • Gel pens (Black, Purple, Gray, Pink, Green, Gold) • Chalk (Gray, Pink, Purple, Green) • Scallop scissors

INSTRUCTIONS:

Page. Trim *Little Baby Faces* to fit and glue on album page.

Title. Cut 2 3/4" Green and 2 1/4" White cardstock strips. Trim bottom of Green with scallop scissors. Glue strips on page. Cut Pink, Green, Lavender and Yellow cardstock letters using template. Outline with matching pens and shade with chalk. Referring to photo for colors and placement, make baby boy and girl. Glue letters and babies on strips.

Journaling. Cut Purple 2 1/4" x 2 3/4", Yellow 2" x 2 1/2" and White 1 3/4" x 2 1/4" cardstock rectangles. Punch corners of White with duck corner. Glue scraps of Lavender, Green and Yellow cardstock behind punches. Layer and glue rectangles together. Apply letter stickers and write 'and' with Black pen.

Buntings. Using pattern, cut Lavender and Green buntings, outline with pens and shade with chalk. Choose photos slightly smaller than buntings, or make photocopies and size as needed. Cut into silhouettes leaving part of blanket showing. Glue bunting edges on page and insert photos. Make rattle and duck as shown. Glue in place.

Baby Love... continued

Baby Boy .

- Peach - 5/16", 3/4" and Purple 3/4" Circles
- Green - 1 1/4" Circle
- White - 5/8" Scallop Heart
- Peach - 5/8" Footprint
- Pink - 1" Smiley
- White - 1/4" Flower

Baby Girl.

- Peach - 5/16", 3/4" and Pink 1 1/4" Circles
- Green - 3/5" Circle
- White - 5/8" Scallop Heart
- Peach - 5/8" Footprint,
- Pink - 1" Smiley Face
- Purple - 1/4" Bow
- Yellow - 1/4" Swirl

Duck.

- Pink - 3/16" Circle
- Black 1/8" Circle
- Yellow 5/8" Circle
- Green - 3/4" Circle
- Yellow - 3/4" and 2 1/4" Heart
- Orange - 1/2" Rectangle
- Black - Swirl Border #4

Rattle.

- Yellow - 5/8", 3/4" and Pink 1 1/4" Circles
- Yellow - 1 1/2" Rectangle
- Green - 7/8" Bow
- Purple - 1/4" Country Heart

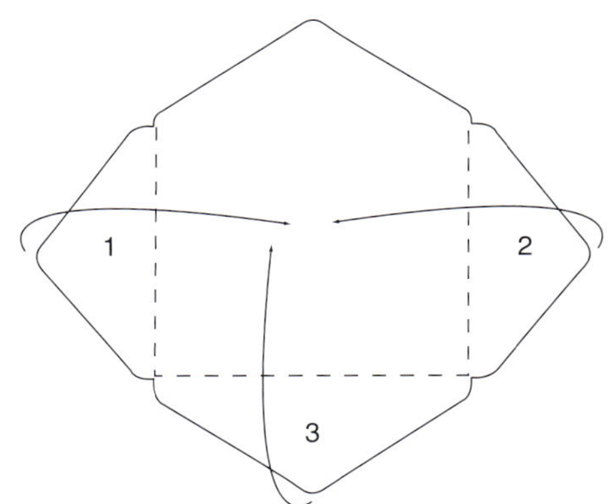

Best Friend

MATERIALS: Design Originals 12" papers (*#0411 Letter Postcards, #0394 Sunflowers*) • Green Print Vellum • 12" Cardstock (White, Green, Light Green, Bright Yellow) • Punches (3/8", 5/8" and 1 1/2" Flower; 1" and 1 1/4" Square; 1/2" Birch Leaf) • Wave Border template • Letter stickers (3/8" and 5/8" Black, Journaling) • Gel pen (Green) • Scallop scissors

INSTRUCTIONS:

Page. Trim *Letter Postcards* paper to fit and glue on album page.

Borders. Cut 1/4" and 3/4" strips of Yellow and 5/8" strip of Green cardstock. Trim Green with scallop scissors. Glue strips on page as shown. Trace wave pattern on Green cardstock using template. Cut into vine shape. Glue on page.

Envelope. Cut envelope back from Light Green cardstock. Cut envelope front from Vellum. Glue Vellum envelope on cardstock and cardstock on page. Decorate border, vine and envelope with a gel pen.

Punch Green, Yellow and Green Vellum squares. Embellish with gel pen. Glue on envelope.

Title. Cut *Sunflowers* paper into squares. Punch floral images with flower punches turned upside down. Punch leaf images with leaf punch. Assemble flowers. Glue leaves and large flowers on vine and small flowers on border and squares. Apply letter stickers.

Photo. Cut 3 7/8" x 5 1/8" Yellow, 3 1/2" x 4 3/4" Green and 3 1/4" x 4 1/2" Light Green cardstock rectangles. Crop photo. Glue cardstock pieces and photo together. Place in envelope.

Journaling. Cut 1 1/4" x 3 1/4" Bright Yellow, 1 1/8" x 3 1/8" Green and 1" x 3" White cardstock rectangles. Glue together and apply journaling sticker. Glue on envelope.

Insert a photo of your best friend in a delicately colored vellum envelope that says she is remembered every day of the year.

Top Dog

MATERIALS: Design Originals 12" paper (*#0403 Doggone Dog Days, #0399 Garden Leaves*) • Flannel paper (Brown, Tan) • Wood texture paper • 12" Cardstock (White, Black, Pink, Dark Pink, Tan, Brown) Punches (1" and 2¼" Circle; ⅝", ⅞" and 2" Heart; ¼", ½", ¾" and 1½" Oval; ⅞" Cat; ⅝" and 1⅜" Bone; 1⅝" Grass; Corner Rounder) • Letter stickers (⅜" White) • Gel pens (Gray, Pink, Brown, Red, White) • Marker (Pink) • Chalk (Brown, Gray) • Two ⅝" wiggle eyes

Man's best friend has earned a page with a doghouse and bones that says he's the 'Top Dog'.

INSTRUCTIONS:

Page. Trim *Doggone Dog Days* to fit and glue on album page. Round corners on 2 photos, glue on page.

Title. Cut 2⅛" wide Dark Pink and 1⅞" wide Pink cardstock strips. Glue on top of page. Punch 1⅜" bones from White cardstock. Trim, outline with Black pen and shade with Gray chalk to make letters. Glue on strips. Punch 2 Tan cats and 4 Brown ¼" ovals. Glue cats on strips, add ovals for ears. Decorate referring to photo.

Doghouse. Cut doghouse and door from Tan cardstock using patterns. Color doghouse with markers and pens. Score and fold door flaps. Glue flaps on doghouse. Cut 3" x 3⅝" dark wood paper rectangle. Cut 2 each light wood ¼" x 3" and ¼" x 3⅝" strips. Glue rectangle and strips on door as shown. Punch 5 Dark Pink ⅞" hearts, 4 Pink ⅝" hearts and ⅝" White bone from cardstock. Outline with Gray pen and shade with Gray chalk. Glue on doghouse.

Plants. Punch eight 1⅝" grass shapes from *Garden Leaves* paper. Layer and glue on sides of doghouse.

Dog Bowl. Cut dog bowl from Pink cardstock using pattern. Outline with Gray pen and shade with Gray chalk. Cut slit in top of bowl. Punch White 1⅜" bone, outline with Gray pen and insert in bowl. Glue bowl on grass. Apply letter stickers. Write date with pen.

Dog Pull-Up. Using template, cut 2¼" photo and and 2⅜" Dark Pink cardstock mat, glue together. From Tan flannel paper, cut 3¾" circle body and punch 2" heart head. From Brown flannel paper, punch 2" heart for ears, three 1" circles for paws and chin and two 1½" ovals for feet. From cardstock, punch Tan ⅞" heart for muzzle, Black ¼" oval for nose, 9 Pink ¼" ovals for tongue and paws, 2 Pink ½" ovals for paws and 2 Black ¾" ovals for eyes. Outline muzzle with Brown and make whiskers with Black pens. Shade with Brown chalk. Assemble dog referring to photo. Insert dog in door.

DOG BOWL PATTERN

DOGHOUSE PATTERN

Pocket Pull-Ups

Here Comes Trouble

MATERIALS: Design Originals 12" papers (*#0404 Cat Escapades, #0399 Garden Leaves*) • 12" Cardstock (White, Peach, Green, Light Green, Cream, Tan, Orange, Gray, Yellow, Pink) • Punches (3⁄16", 1¼" and 2¼" Circle; ½", ¾", 5⁄16", 1¼" and 1¾" Oval; ½", 7⁄8" and 1½" Rectangle; ½" Birch Leaf; 2" Star; 5⁄8" Pawprint; 9⁄16" Flower; 5⁄8" Fleur de Lis; ¼" Cat; 15⁄8" Grass; 2" Maple Leaf; Corner Rounder; Clayson Colossal Corner) • Circle template • Letter stickers (3⁄16" Black, 3⁄8" Yellow, ¾" Yellow and Brown, 9⁄16" Number Blocks) • Gel pens (Black, Brown, Gray, Green) • Chalk (Rust, Gray, Brown) • Zig zag edge scissors

INSTRUCTIONS:

Page. Cut *Cat Escapades* paper to fit and glue on album page. Cut a 1¾" wide Yellow cardstock strip, trim edges with scissors. Cut a 1½" wide White cardstock strip. Glue strips together. Glue diagonally to album page and trim ends. Apply ¾" Yellow and Brown and 3⁄16" Black letter stickers.

Page Photo. Cut 4½" Tan, 4¼" Light Green and 41⁄8" Cream cardstock squares. Punch corners of Cream with Colossal Corner and Cat punches. Glue Orange cardstock behind Cats. Punch corners of photo with Corner Rounder. Glue photo and squares together and on page.

Fence. Cut fence from White cardstock and draw pickets with Gray gel pen and ruler. Score and fold gate and flaps. Glue fence on bottom of page. Test gate movement. Glue photo behind gate and apply Yellow letter and number block stickers to back of gate.

Sign. Punch a 1½" rectangle and cut a ¼" x 3" strip from Tan cardstock. Trim ends of rectangle with wavy scissors. Detail sign and handle with Brown and Gray pens and shade with Brown chalk. Glue together and apply 3⁄16" Black letter stickers.

Flowers & Grass. Punch grass from *Garden Leaves* paper. Punch flowers from Yellow, centers from Light Green, and leaves from Green cardstock. Cut stems from Green. Outline and detail flowers with Brown and centers and grass with Green pens. Glue sign, flowers and grass in place.

Hinges & Latch. Punch 2 Gray 7⁄8" Rectangles and 4 Gray fleur de lis. Glue on gate to form hinges. Punch ½" Gray rectangle, and glue for latch. Outline shapes with Black pen.

Cat. From Peach cardstock, cut a 4" circle and punch a 2¼" circle for head, two 1¼" circles for front paws, two 1¾" ovals for back paws, star for ears and maple leaf for ruff. Punch 1¼" White oval for muzzle and 2 each of 5⁄16" Green, ½" White and ¾" Black ovals for eyes. Punch Pink pawprint for nose. For paw pads, punch 8 Gray 5⁄16" ovals and 2 Gray ½" ovals. Outline and detail Peach pieces with Gray pen and shade with Rust chalk. Add stripes with Brown and inner ears with Gray pens. Shade muzzle with Rust and nose and eyes with Gray chalk. Cut 23⁄8" circle photo. Assemble cat referring to photo. Crop cat photo into 2¼" circle. Glue to cat. Insert cat in fence.

GATE

Trouble comes in all shapes and sizes… cats to little boys. Remember your favorite 'double troubles' on a page filled with feline fun.

Pocket Pull-Ups

Love Letters

MATERIALS: Design Originals 12" paper (*#0418 Love Letters, #0416 Diamonds on Ivory, #0391 Antique Shoes*) • Pink mulberry paper • 12" Cardstock (Burgundy, Green, Light Brown, Gold, Ivory) • Punches (1/4" and 1 1/2" Circle; 1", 1 1/4" and 1 1/2" Square; 2 3/8" Contemporary Heart, Hanover Heritage Square Corner; Crown Border) • Heart template • Letter stickers (1 1/2" Burgundy Block, Burgundy Journaling) • Wavy edge scissors • Plastic buttons and charms • Gold and Burgundy tassels • Letters to place in tag • 1 1/2" round metal rim tag • Wire cutters

INSTRUCTIONS:

Page. Cut 2 1/2" wide strip of *Love Letters* paper, glue on album page. Cut a 7 1/2" wide piece of Burgundy cardstock. Trim one edge with wavy scissors, glue on page. Cut a 7" wide piece of Green cardstock and glue on page.

Title. Punch 1 1/4" Burgundy and 1 1/2" Green squares. Trim Green squares to 1 1/8" x 1 1/2" and trim stickers to fit. Apply stickers. Glue squares together and on page.

Pocket. Cut mulberry paper to 5 1/4" x 8". Spray lightly with water before tearing edges. Separate tough fibers with scissors. Let dry and glue on page.

Glue *Diamonds on Ivory* paper on Ivory cardstock. Trace shipping tag pattern and cut out. Trace string hole on Brown cardstock. Cut out. Glue pieces together. Punch 1/4" circle for string hole. Thread tassel through hole, tie knot and trim excess thread. Score and fold sides and bottom of shipping tag. Glue on mulberry paper.

Using template, trace a 3 1/2" heart on *Love Letters* paper and a 2 1/2" heart on Burgundy cardstock. Punch a contemporary heart from *Love Letters*. Glue hearts together and on tag.

Punch a 1/2" circle from *Love Letters* paper, glue to metal rim tag. Glue rim on shipping tag.

Cut images from *Antique Shoes* paper. Glue on tags. Cut backs off buttons with wire cutters. Glue buttons and charms on tags.

Punch corners of Burgundy cardstock with corner punch. Cut off corners and glue on Light Brown cardstock, cut again. Glue corners on page. Punch Gold borders, glue in place.

Cut 1 3/4" x 2 1/4" Burgundy and 1 5/8" x 2 1/8" Light Brown rectangles. Glue together and apply journaling sticker. Glue on page.

Store your treasured letters in an elegant pocket decorated with charms and fancy papers.

BOX BACK

I Am So Fortunate

MATERIALS: Design Originals 12" paper *(#0405 Fortune Cookies)* • Red Vellum • 12" Cardstock (White, 2 Black, Red, Tan) • Punches ($\frac{1}{4}$" Circle; $1\frac{5}{8}$" Tulip; $2\frac{1}{4}$" Oval; 1" Good Luck Frame) • Square and Oval templates • Letter stickers ($\frac{3}{8}$" Red, $\frac{5}{16}$" Red and White) • Gel pens (Black, Brown) • Chalk (Brown)

INSTRUCTIONS:

Page. Trim Black cardstock to fit and glue on album page. Cut $2\frac{1}{8}$" wide and $\frac{1}{4}$" wide strips of Red cardstock. Cut a $2\frac{1}{8}$" wide strip of *Fortune Cookie* paper. Punch $2\frac{1}{8}$" Red strip with 7 good luck frames. Glue paper strips on page as shown.

Title. Punch Red cardstock tulips. Referring to diagram, cut strips for letters. Glue letters on page. Apply White letters to complete the title.

Frame. Cut $6\frac{5}{8}$" x $9\frac{1}{2}$" White cardstock. Score and make fold in center. Cut four $\frac{1}{8}$" Black strips, glue on door frame and cut off excess. Glue door frame on page.

Pocket. Trace box front with flaps and box back with lid on Red Vellum, cut out. Score and fold flaps. Glue flaps on back of box to form pocket. Glue on front of door frame. Crop photo to fit in pocket and insert. Punch 2 Tan ovals. Trim fortune cookie referring to pattern. Outline edges with Brown pen and shade with Brown chalk. Cut a fortune from Fortune Cookie paper. Glue edges of cookie on pocket and insert fortune.

Photos. Crop and mat additional photos with Red cardstock and F*ortune Cookie* paper. Glue inside door frame. Cut $\frac{3}{4}$" x 3" Red and $\frac{1}{2}$" x $2\frac{3}{4}$" White cardstock strips. Glue together and write names with Black pen. Cut $1\frac{1}{8}$" x $2\frac{1}{2}$" Fortune Cookie and Black cardstock and $\frac{3}{4}$" x $2\frac{1}{8}$" White cardstock strips. Punch edges of Black with $\frac{1}{4}$" circle. Glue strips together and apply Red letter stickers.

BOX FRONT

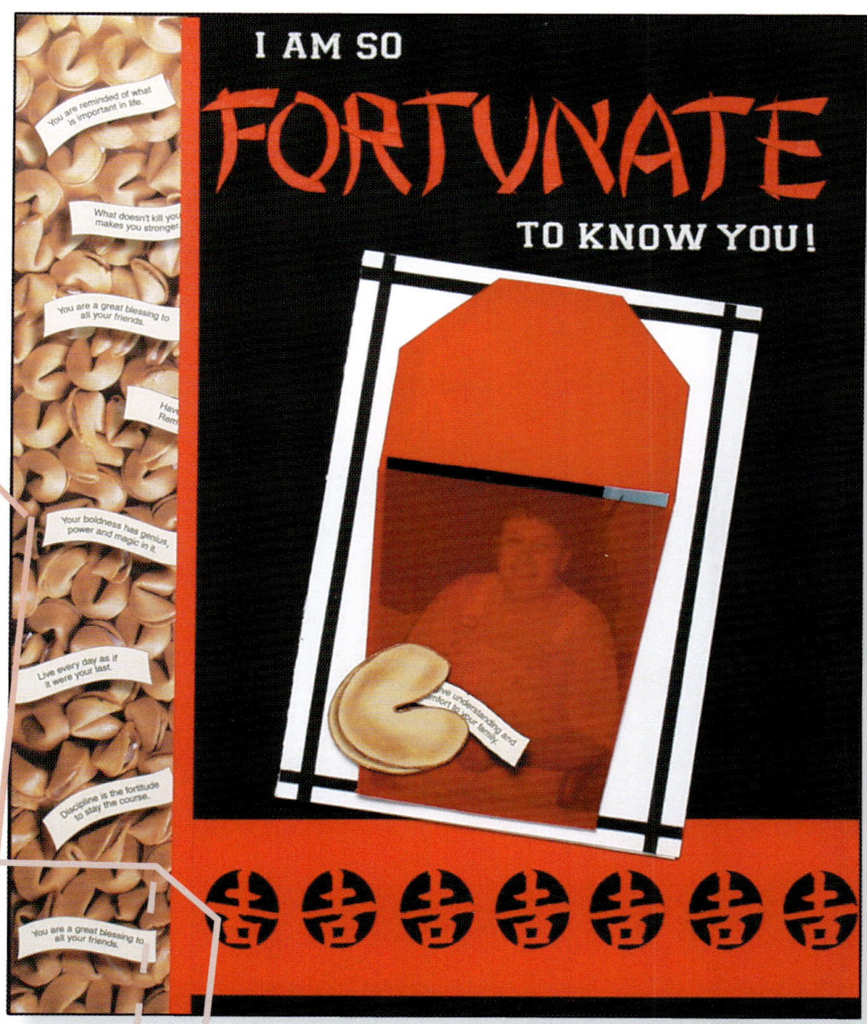

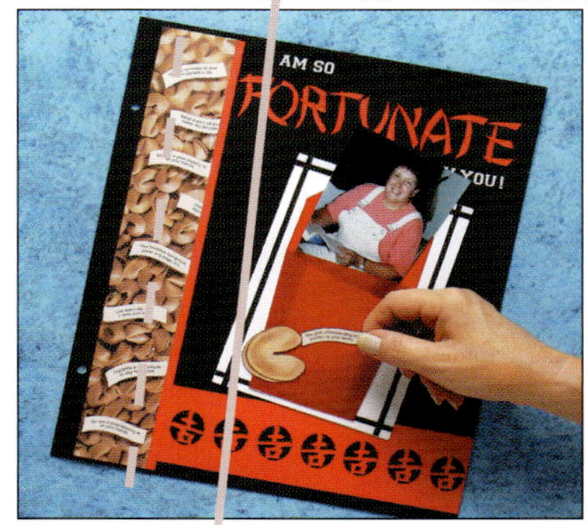

Anyone is fortunate who shares a loving relationship with family or a friend. Honor that relationship with a page that states your feeling.

You are a great blessing to all your friends.

What doesn't kill you makes you stronger.

Live every day as if it were your last.

Discipline is the fortitude to stay the course.

Folding Slider

"and Baby Makes Three..."

Lift the door to see a happy couple and pull the slider to see the baby.

Punch cardstock and paper as follows:

Mama Bear.
Tan - Two 1/2" circle ears
Tan - 1" circle head
Tan - 1 1/2" heart cut in half for arms
Tan - Two 1 1/4" heart feet
Purple Print - 1 1/2" heart shirt
White - 1 1/2" scallop oval skirt
White - 5/8" scallop heart collar
Brown - 1/4" heart nose
Pink - 1/4" bow

Papa Bear.
Tan - Two 1/2" circle ears
Tan - 1" circle head
Tan - 1 1/2" heart cut in half for arms
Tan - Two 1 1/4" heart feet
Tan - 1 1/2" heart body
Purple - 1 1/2" Print heart vest
Brown - 1/4" heart nose
Green - 1/2" Print bow for tie

Baby Bear.
Tan - Two 5/16" circle ears
Tan - 3/4" circle head
Tan - 7/8" heart cut in half for arms
Tan - 1 1/8" heart body
White - 1 1/8" heart diaper
Tan - Two 7/8" heart feet
Brown - 1/8" heart nose
Pink - 1/16" circle for pacifier
Blue - 3/16" circle for pacifier

MATERIALS: Design Originals 12" paper *(#0402 Little Baby Faces, Green Print, Purple Prints)* • Cardstock (Black, White, Tan, Brown, Green, Yellow, Purple, Lavender, Pink, Blue) • Stickers (3/8" Black, 3/8" White, 3/8" Red letters, 3/4" Purple numbers) • Punches (1/16", 1/8", 3/16", 5/16", 1/2", 3/4", 1", 1 1/4" and 2" Circles; 1/8", 3/16", 7/8", 1 1/8", 1 1/4" and 1 1/2" Hearts; 5/8" Scallop Heart; 1 1/2" Scallop Oval; 1/2" Bow) • 1" letter template • Gel pens (Brown, Black) • Chalk (Green, Pink, Yellow, Purple, Brown, Gray)

INSTRUCTIONS:

Page. Trim *Little Baby Faces* paper and glue on page.

Borders. Cut 2 Purple 2" wide and 2 White 1 3/4" wide strips of cardstock. Cut wavy edges, glue on page. To make letters, punch 1" and 1 1/4" circles using Purple, Green, Pink and Yellow cardstock. Trim. Punch 3/16" holes. Shade with matching chalk. Outline and make stitches with a Black pen. Glue on borders. Add 1/8" Black circles.

Frame. Cut a 5 1/2" x 7" Black rectangle, glue on page. Make a Green cardstock door. Punch the center of the right edge with a 2" circle. Make a 'Slider' with Black and Pink cardstock. Apply Black, White and Red letter stickers.

Cut 4" x 4 3/4" Yellow and 3 3/4" x 4 1/2" Lavender rectangles. Punch Lavender with bear mountain corners. Glue scraps of Blue and Pink cardstock behind the corners. Glue mats on the front of door and slip a photo in the corner pockets.

Finish. Shade bear clothing with matching chalk. Make cheeks and inner ears with Pink chalk. Add details with a Black pen. Glue bears inside the door. Add number stickers.